Thank you!
Enjoy these recipes
Cheers!
Gloria

The Pork Chop in the Window

The Pork Chop in the Window

Gloria Carnevale

The Round House Press
Kent, Connecticut

The Round House Press
P. O. Box 744
Kent, Connecticut 06757
info@TheRoundHousePress.com

ISBN: 978-0-9823089-9-8

Carnevale, Gloria.
The pork chop in the window / Gloria Carnevale. -- Kent, Connecticut
: The Round House Press, [2014]
pages ; cm.
ISBN: 978-0-9823089-9-8
Summary: More than thirty honest-to-cholesterol, politically incorrect
recipes, all family favorites from the never-boring test kitchens of the
author's insanely insatiable family, spanning cultures and generations.
As a record of her family's tendency toward wacky mealtime adventures,
the author describes her book as a guide to the lost art of Eating-While-
Laughing-Without-Choking, with something here that every reader can
identify with, be it family members or recipes.--Publisher.
1. Cooking, Italian. 2. Italian American families--Food. 3. Italian
American families--Humor. 4. Dinners and dining--Humor. 5. Cook-
books. I. Title.

TX723 .C37 2014		2014951502
641.5945--dc23		1411

Printed in the United States of America
Cover illustration and design: Scott Bricher
Book design: raqoon-design.com

Contents

*To my family, who empowered us by making each one
feel special and very loved*

Love you, Lou, Alex, and Stephanie

Introduction

If you have any sense, you're probably asking yourself the same question I'm asking myself: Why must there be yet another Italian cookbook? I mean, there's Nonni's cookbook, my mother's favorite Italian recipes, cooking with Lidia, Mario, and Giada, even a cookbook dedicated to the Mafia, for crying out loud!

After giving this cookbook idea much thought, I decided to go ahead and write the darn thing, primarily because I needed to, but also to record some of the craziest cooking experiences that I've had since I was a small child. Some of these experiences I saw as an observer, and for some I was the chef.

Another Italian cookbook sprinkled with stories of warm, crusty bread right out of the hearth? Another meatball mastery manual? Another Italian cookbook about sauce being stirred while the cement shoes are drying and the fish is wrapped in oily paper? No, instead I see *The Pork Chop in the Window* as a guide to a lost art that this uptight world of ours is missing— I call it The-Art-of-Eating-While-Laughing-Without-Choking, a tradition my family could easily offer a webinar on.

Many of these recipes aren't just Italian, they span cultures and generations. And from what I hear, my family's tendency toward wacky mealtime adventures is hardly limited to our DNA. I am certain that readers everywhere can, and will, connect to one or more of this *Pork Chop's* chapters, family members, or recipes. After all, wherever we live or whomever we invite to our table, food is the great equalizer in life!

As a member of a rather large and delightfully dysfunctional family, I feel privileged to let you in on our laughable lunches and demented dinners, allowing you, the reader, to share a good laugh with a family that never seems capable of a boring meal.

So sit back, crank up the oven, refresh yourself on the Heimlich Maneuver, enjoy the ride... and above all... *mangia!*

Chapter 1: Funerals

Ever since I can remember, dying meant fried veal cutlets.

Immediately following the news that someone had bit the big one, the aunts, all five of them, would go into high-gear frying mode as soon as my cousin made the pilgrimage down the street to the butcher for the best grain-fed veal. Then the assembly-line frying would begin. One aunt would dip the veal cutlet into the egg, and another would dip it into the breadcrumbs. It would then be ceremoniously dropped into the cast-iron frying pan's olive oil, browned on both sides and drained on a paper towel that had been placed on a plate.

They'd make a *mountain* of veal cutlets, and the histrionics that ensued during this process are etched into my mind forever.

For example, when my cousin died of a rare cancer after serving as a Marine in Vietnam, one of my aunts swore it was because the food he'd eaten wasn't clean, and so she got the idea that ALL food needed to be washed. So the veal cutlets were washed before they got dipped, breaded, and fried. I am not kidding. She washed everything. Fish, meat, poultry, everything got douched (that was my sister's word for it).

The aunts were also firm believers in vinegar; they even polished the furniture with a solution of vinegar and water. "Mom's douching the furniture," is what my sister would say.

Of course we—my parents, siblings, and I—lived an hour-and-a-half away from this three-ring circus of clowns, and I would have a hard time waiting until the calling hours and the funeral were over to enjoy the veal cutlets. It was killing me that the cousins were already there, diving in.

The best was when it was one of the aunts or uncles who died (there were *lots* of them with heart problems). When that happened, my mother would want to "get there early to help the others do the frying." Oh, happy day, when I got to go and watch this show, and get a cutlet right from the pan! Thank you, heart disease! It sounds heartless (please forgive the pun) but those cutlets were always *so good*. There's nothing like a nice hot fried veal cutlet, pure and simple, straight from the pan. Forget the sauce and mozzarella; veal parmesan is overrated, especially since a lousy sauce can destroy the entire cutlet.

Oh, and sometimes throughout this book you'll read the word "fresh" the way I always heard it, loud and clear, so you got the point. "He makes it *fressshh*" the aunts would say about the cheese man who made mozzarella, always hanging onto the end of the word. "Go to the bakery and get *fressshh* bread," they'd order any cousin not engaged in child labor at that moment.

Funeral Veal Cutlets
Serves 4 to 6

50 lbs. of *freshhhh* prime-cut veal (okay, not
    50 pounds, but you get the idea)
2 pounds of veal cutlets
2 whole eggs beaten with water
1 ½ cups Progresso seasoned breadcrumbs
    (other brands are fine if they are seasoned
    as well)
½ cup virgin olive oil

Dip each cutlet into the egg and water mixture, then dip into the breadcrumbs.

Heat a large cast iron skillet and add 1/8 cup of olive oil (you will need to add more as the cutlets fry and absorb the oil).

When the oil is frying hot, put the veal cutlets into the pan and fry on both sides until golden brown.

Drain on paper towels.

Chapter 2: Not to Worry, We're in God's Country

The bunch of them were nuts, plain and simple. The aunts never forgave my father for taking their baby sister, Mindi, up to God's Country, New York. Better she should have stayed in the 'hood of Newark, New Jersey in a three-room apartment.

But they made the best of what they called a *BAAAAAD* situation. (They leaned on the word "bad" the same way they said "fresssssh," always hanging on the "a" a little longer than usual for effect.) Nevertheless, they'd always manage to make the pilgrimage upstate on a Saturday, much to the horror of my dad. Seriously, they'd pull up in Uncle Joe's big-ass Cadillac, loaded down with the goodies that they thought we couldn't get here in New York: loaves of decent bread, olive-oil-soaked peppers, provolone-stuffed olives, Tasty Cakes (had to have THEM), and of course, Charms hard candies. (Aunt Santa—more about her later—worked for the Charms Company and had stock options in the 1940s, so we had Charms hard candies until 1971, when she blessedly ran out of them.)

But, back to the reason they would visit. The secret was *gardunes*. You know, the green dandelion leaves you see before the yellow flowers take over. The aunts lived for a nice gardune salad. In their world, food was always "nice," as in "Have a nice meatball" or "Have a nice piece of cake." Never once did I hear them say, "Have a mean slice of roast beef." Food was *nice*.

They'd arrive, armed not only with food, but also with pocket knives. I swear Aunt Bianca had a switchblade. Right after that healthy lunch of capa di colla, prosciutto, provolone, and oil-soaked everything, it was time to search and destroy. The aunts would arm themselves with their weapons and paper bags to collect the booty, and it was up to me to take them to wherever the tastiest gardunes were. And no matter how hard I tried to steer them into the woods, they would end up in the residential development, digging up total strangers' lawns.

Most of the time this upset me greatly. Hell, I rode the school bus with these kids, and it was left for me to explain why my family wanted to duff up their lawns like a golfer gone wild. It was a mortifying experience, and they never apologized. Why would they? "We're in God's Country, it's okay."

A *Nice* Gardune Salad

Pick enough dandelion leaves to make a salad
Olive oil
Balsamic vinegar
Salt and pepper

Pick the "gardunes" early in the spring, so they are tender—and try to stay on your own property, for safety's sake.

Clean them really well—every dog and cat will have pissed on your lawn the night before.

Put them into a bowl and mix with olive oil, vinegar, salt and pepper, and eat. I think balsamic vinegar is best because it is not so acidic, and adds a nice flavor to the savory gardunes.

Chapter 3: Save Me a Meatball

I'll confess: I didn't plan on giving out a recipe for meatballs, but this one holds a special place in my heart, and the story *must* be told.

My Aunt Bianca made THE BEST meatballs in the world. No kidding, she was the master meatball maker. Cousins from South Jersey would beg their parents to take a ride to her house on a Sunday morning (after all, when else would you fry a meatball?). *Fried* is what I said. The word almost seems vulgar, by today's standards of health, but who knew back then—or cared?

We, the black sheep family members who jumped ship to live *upstate,* even we *had* to drive ninety miles to taste these spheres straight from heaven.

But first, we had to attend Mass at our parish church. Then my dad would have to drive all of us home, so that we could change our clothes, gather what we were bringing with us, and check the house FIVE HUNDRED TIMES to make sure that the door was locked (I told you they were all nuts). Normally, I could care less. Except when it came to meatballs.

The cousins would be already there, way ahead of us, eating up all of the deliciousness, hot and oily, right from the frying pan. I hated them, and I hated living upstate for this reason alone. Our upstate black sheep family would always blow into Aunt Bianca's house just as the evil cousins were wiping the grease off their lips. Garlic smells permeated the house. "Oh, I saved each of you a meatball before I threw them into the sauce." Yeah, thanks.

When I was old enough to drive, you can bet I would race my fat butt down there extra early so as to be the first one to get a meatball hot out of the pan. Lucky for me, too, because during those times I made sure to be a good study, watching every move my aunt made in the development of the perfect meatball.

I no longer fry my meatballs (thanks for nothing, Doc), but my recipe turns out the same, either way: fried or baked. You choose which you would prefer. Fry and die? Hey, you only live once, and you *need* to taste these. Trust me.

Kick-ass Meatballs
Serves 4 to 6

Chopped sirloin (2 pounds makes about 12-15
meatballs, so buy accordingly)
Eggs (1 egg per pound of meat)
4 tablespoons dried parsley
1 ½ cups Progresso seasoned breadcrumbs per
2 pounds chopped meat
½ cup parmesan cheese per 2 pounds meat
One tablespoon garlic powder

Throw everything into a large bowl and mix really
well with your hands. I mean really well to get the fla-
vors to meld.

Then, heat a large cast iron skillet (déjà-vu?) and
add olive oil.

Fry those bad boys until they are browned and the
smell makes you intoxicated and salivating.

Drain on paper towels, eat hot from the pan, OR
put whatever is left into the sauce you made for dinner!

Chapter 4: Bon Voyage, Gertrude

"Man the lifeboats, Jersey's coming," is what my dad would say when the family would make their pilgrimage to upstate New York.

Uncle Herbie worked as a food inspector, specifically in bakeries. His weekly job was to inspect the cleanliness of the establishments and close them down if they didn't meet Board of Health standards. Use your imagination as to how that went. Every week he was *showered* with pastries, cakes, pies, cookies, bread, biscotti, you name it, to take home to his family. And take it home he did. LOTS of it. We were never without a dessert (or ten, for that matter) at any given gathering. We got to be discerning, too, about certain ones. Like the grain pies that we had at Easter time. They were a mixture of cornmeal/polenta with citron and God-knows-what-else in them. No one liked them, but we tasted them just because we had them to taste. *Taste* was another all-time favorite word of the aunts. "Take a taste," or "Just taste it," they'd say. God forbid you really liked it and did more than taste. That's what happened to my dad, which you can read about in a future chapter.

So, in 1977 my parents celebrated their twenty-fifth wedding anniversary. My siblings and I decided to give them a surprise party, and my aunt said that Uncle Herbie would bring the anniversary cake. My sister and I thought *No good can come of this*, but we didn't want to hurt his feelings, so...

They arrived early in the afternoon, my cousin Junie in white patent leather shoes (he didn't get the memo that in upstate New York you didn't wear white after Labor Day), and enough jewelry to open a Kay's, with the rest of them spilling out of their Lincolns, Buicks, and Cadillacs (Uncle Joe in his brand new one) to enjoy the country, as they called it. Uncle Herbie got out of his Buick and opened the trunk, with my Aunt Santa right up his butt.

Not missing a beat, she plucked a decorator's tube of blue frosting from her bag. My first thought was the usual *No good can come of this,* but I waited for her to say something.

"Oh, the cake got a little messed up, but don't worry, we'll just fix it with this tube of frosting," is the explanation.

As she opened the box, and I swear on my parents, this is the absolute truth, my sister and I saw a cake in the shape of a cruise ship with the words *Bon Voyage, Gertrude* written in big letters on it. I stood there long enough to see my sister pass out in the driveway, as my aunt is saying, "Ooooh, Uncle Herbie got the cake for free. All we have to do is take a knife and smooth the words out, and we can write *Happy Anniversary* with this frosting."

We managed to shipwreck Gertrude, but the green frosting mixed with the blue turned a murky brown, and the cake looked like it had washed up on the shores of the Mississippi.

The aunts still insisted it was a *nice* cake, and we should *taste* it.

No good came of this.

Chapter 5: Millie Cake

My father's family was no exception when it came to crazy, either. In fact, they may have invented the word. Interestingly enough, their culinary tastes pretty much leaned toward turkey tetrazzini and buttered white bread bologna sandwiches. Maybe they were only masquerading as Italians. I couldn't tell.

However, it was Cousin Millie who defended the family's honor in the culinary department. Millie could make a cake that would bring tears of happiness to the eyes of the Cake Boss. The family called it Millie Cake, and there was a ceremony attached to its presentation and serving. *Of course there was.*

We only got Millie Cake on special occasions, which were Christmas and birthdays. I was extra lucky, because my birthday is a week after Christmas. Score one for me.

Millie would also make a tray of cream puffs, Millie-style, for those who wanted a *taste* (okay, that word wasn't only used by the Jersey clan). In any case, Millie Cake had to be brought to the table ceremoniously, and its journey began across a main highway, where it sat in Millie's kitchen.

After the dishes were cleared from the table and brought into the kitchen, and the coffee was set up, it was time for Millie to ask The Big Question, "Who is coming with me to help?"

Now, things could get fooky during the winter months, when the roads were treacherous and the slightest wrong move could end in disaster, since we would have to walk across that highway and down the road in order to get to the cake and cream puffs, which were waiting patiently in Millie's refrigerator for their debut and demise.

I was always chosen to help, and I must say, never once was there drama involved. We'd go to her house, get the cake (which, by the way, was displayed on a cake pedestal), and the cream puffs, and carefully make our way back down the road, across the highway, and to my parents' house, where the ceremony really began to get serious.

The cake carrier would walk into the dining room to the oohs and aahs of the liquored up fools seated at the table, followed by the cream puff carrier and the sounds of "OMG, cream puffs, too?" like they didn't know she'd make them. *Seriously*, you *knew* there would be cream puffs, nitwits.

And then, the cake-cutting part of the ceremony. Millie would wield a porcelain handled knife… pink, of course, with little white and pink flowers on it, used especially to cut Millie Cake. She'd cut a circle in the middle of the cake so as to make even slices. Now I know this sounds crazy, but no one *ever* ate the middle. It would sit in the refrigerator for days until the cream got hard and the cake drooped and my mother finally threw it out. Crazy.

The diners would descend upon that cake like starving seven-year locusts and would eat that cake like it was their job, washing it down with a few cream puffs for good measure. I guess if your weekly diet consisted of buttered white bread bologna sandwiches, you'd wolf a good cake down, too.

Millie Cake was indigenous to Millie, and although Millie is long gone and no one has the exact recipe, I can describe from memory what it tasted and looked like:

A Millie Cake Memory

Eight layers of rich, dense, spongy yellow cake, each layer separated by heavy whipped cream, flecked with tiny chocolate shavings. Approximate height of cake: ten inches. The total cake was engulfed in a one-to-two-inch layer of heavy whipped cream, topped with swirls of pink (for the birthday girls) or blue (for the boys).

If it wasn't a birthday cake, then the top of the cake would be topped with chocolate curls so thin that they resembled joint papers. They melted in your mouth upon entry.

Dear reader, please don't get mad and throw the book at this point. Trust me, I have truly tried to recreate this cake, but my pitiful efforts have been in vain. The Millie Cake recipe went when Millie did.

I am giving you the recipe for Millie Cream Puffs to assuage the pain.

Millie Cream Puffs

This *should* serve 8 to 10, but see the note at the bottom of this recipe for further instructions.

> 1/2 cup water
> 4 tablespoons unsalted butter
> ½ cup flour
> 2 eggs

Preheat the oven to 375 degrees.

Combine the water and butter in a saucepan and bring it to a boil. Remove from heat at the same time as you add the flour, stirring vigorously with a wooden spoon. Return to medium heat and continue stirring until dough leaves the sides of the pan and forms a ball. Add the eggs, one at a time, beating really hard until the dough is smooth.

Place large rounded tablespoons of dough onto an ungreased cookie sheet, 2 inches apart. Bake for 30 minutes or until the puffs are golden brown. Carefully cut each puff in half and scoop out the centers, leaving them on a rack to cool.

While they are cooling, make the filling:

> 1 pint heavy cream
> ½ cup confectioner's sugar
> 1 teaspoon vanilla or any flavor liquor (I like
>   using Grand Marnier or Kahlua)

Beat all ingredients with electric beaters on high until the cream is whipped and hard peaks form. Fill each puff with cream. Refrigerate immediately and keep refrigerated until ready to be eaten.

This recipe makes 10 to 12 cream puffs, so I like to double it. The vultures eat them two-fisted.

Chapter 6: Bring Me the Head of John the Baptist

I haven't gotten into the names of the crazy aunts, but I'm sure you noticed the name of Aunt Santa. She got her name because my grandparents couldn't decide on a saint's name, so they just called her "Saint." Makes perfect sense. Aunt Columbia got her name because… you guessed it! She was born on Columbus Day. My cousin Lucia Jean got her name because she was born on St. Lucy's day. The list goes on and on, and is a story in itself. Thank heavens no one was born on St. Vitus Day. They'd have to dance their way through life. Pay attention; there will be a test later on.

What I'm talking about here is Easter Sunday. Did we have antipasti? Of course. Some kind of lasagna with meatballs? Certainly. Were there braccioles simmering in wine and mushrooms on the stove? Absolutely. So then what's the big deal? Well, we also had capo di agnello . *The whole thing*. With a mint-infused orange stuffed into its mouth.

For those of you who are frantically googling the term, stop right there, I'll 'fess up. It's a lamb's head. Remember Shari Lewis and her puppet LambChop? Yup, you got it.

What Italian family didn't have capo di agnello for Easter? Plenty, is my guess. They fasted and penanced their way through Lent and Holy Week like Gandhi in the 1960s to prepare themselves for this Easter Feast. My cousin Elaine was the poor sucker who had to go to the butcher's the day after Ash Wednesday to order the lamb, then again on Holy Saturday to go and fetch it. I always wondered why she seemed a little unglued her whole life. Hey, if you entered a butcher shop in downtown Newark, New Jersey and saw the horrors she did, unglued would be an understatement. "Jimmy the Knife," as the butcher was called, kept everything hanging so that my aunts, and the rest of the nutty women like them, could see that everything was *freshhhhh*.

Elaine would carry the carcass (because buying the whole thing was cheaper, and they were all about a bargain) the six blocks from the butcher shop to her apartment, up three flights of stairs, then dump it on the back porch to await its journey across town to my Aunt Bianca's house.

Around three o'clock in the afternoon, my Uncle Sal would pull up in his big-ass Chevy and go upstairs, licking his lips all the way up to the three-room apartment with the porch where lay our Easter main feature. My aunt Ann would let him in, and he'd make his way up the stairs to her fridge. Scooping up the carcass, he'd cheerfully say "See you tomorrow," carting the lamb down three flights of stairs to dump it into the back seat of the Chevy. Then he'd blow down the avenue to his house across town.

Aunt Bianca, who'd be waiting for him in the kitchen, would call out, "Sal! Put it on the back porch" as soon as she heard him. The back porches attached to all of their houses were like meat lockers anyway, so refrigeration was no problem.

The next morning, while I was at Mass upstate, wondering who was already eating fried meatballs (see Chapter 3), my aunt would begin the preparation of the guest of honor, LambChop. Cooking space was no problem, since they had a stove downstairs in the basement. (Of course they did.) My uncle had purchased a large metal trough-like vessel that could hold the fifteen-pound lamb with no problem, and there it sat while my aunt rubbed it all over with rosemary and olive oil, sticking a few lemons in the back end, and an orange with mint leaves in its mouth.

Uncle Sal would then carry it ceremoniously downstairs to the oven, where it was destined to roast slowly until dinner. The descent of the relatives would begin around one p.m., except for the evil cousins who lived nearby, who could walk to my aunt's house for their *fried* meatballs.

The feasting would begin, first with the antipasto, and on to the pasta, bracciole, and so on. Then Uncle Sal would go downstairs to get the agnello out of the oven, to be served with roasted red potatoes and broccoli rabe. The smells were intoxicating as they wafted closer and closer until the lamb was at the table.

I can never forget the adults' faces as my aunt would carve up the pieces that were each aunt or uncle's personal favorite. "Give me a piece of the cheek," Uncle

Arthur would say. "I'll take some leg," Aunt Yola would order. Their faces actually *shone* with happiness.

As for me, I always liked a nice (see chapter two about *nice* food) piece of lamb, but as I got older I had problems with eating it that grew into an allergy to lamb.

Many years later, married and with two small children, my husband and I decided to spend Easter at an Italian resort in the Catskills. They did everything with the same traditions we enjoyed at home: the Good Friday fish dinner, the Caesar Night on Holy Saturday with the fruit and nut trays, and the seventeen courses. We were enjoying ourselves tremendously, when the waitress approached our table and announced that they were making capo di agnello for Easter dinner the following day, and she was taking orders for the head only for our table, if we wanted to order one.

My husband looked at me wistfully, whispering, "Please?"

"Do you remember what Salome asked for?" I queried.

"But it's Easter." Puppy dog face.

"The kids will be traumatized."

"You weren't!" Sardonic smile.

"How do you know?"

"I know because when you tell the story of the LambChop ceremony you laugh," he says. Hopeful face.

"That's hysterical laughter. The answer is no."

They came around during breakfast on Easter

morning to ask once again, but I stood firm. At dinner that afternoon, we watched as many LambChops made their way to tables of loud, full-of-food-in-their-mouths Italians.

My kids were appalled at the sight of herds of sheep's heads being led to the slaughtermouths, but they quickly forgot about it when large chocolate bunny rabbits were brought to the tables.

In retrospect, I guess the lambs and bunnies met a similar demise.

Maybe a lamb molé stew could be made with the leftovers of both?

Shari Lewis Lamb Special
(okay, the real name for this dish is
Casciotto al Basilico or, Lamb with Basil)

5 cups basil leaves, roughly chopped
2 garlic cloves, roughly chopped
1 boneless leg of lamb, 3 ½-4 pounds
Salt
Freshly ground black pepper
1 tablespoon virgin olive oil
½ cup any dry white wine

Preheat oven to 400 degrees.

Finely chop basil and garlic together.

Open lamb like a book and place on a work surface. Season with salt and pepper.

Spread 2/3 of basil mixture over lamb, roll up, and secure at 2-inch intervals with kitchen twine.

Using a small, sharp knife, cut several 1–inch-deep slits in top of lamb, spacing them apart.

Insert remaining basil mixture into slits and season outside with salt and pepper.

Place lamb in roasting pan and drizzle with oil. Pour wine into pan and cover tightly with foil.

Roast, basting occasionally and resealing with foil. Roast for about 1 hour 15 minutes, or until thermometer reads 140 in thickest part for medium.

Transfer lamb to cutting board and let rest for 10 minutes.

Skim juices from pan. Slice lamb and serve with juice.

Now, if you're not willing to cook a lamb, for whatever reason, but you want to get the full Italian Easter experience, just go to any Italian bakery and buy a large chocolate lamb, place on a platter, sprinkle jellybeans, marshmallow chicks, and so on around it, and serve it to the liquored-up fools who will assuredly mistake it for the real thing, and gobble every chocolately bit of it up. Trust me, I've seen it happen.

Chapter 7: Coffee and Biscotti

As I got older, I realized that this pack of nuts were all about dry, stale cookies. I wanted a *nice,* soft Toll House chocolate chip to go with my milk after school, but NOOOOOO, that's what *the other kids* ate. And, of course, the aunts said the words *other kids* slowly, accentuating every consonant and vowel, so that we'd be sure to get the message.

Anyway, the aunts lived on coffee and biscotti. One aunt swore she improved her diet by adding cigarettes—probably because tobacco starts out as a green plant. There wasn't a house in Jersey that I knew of that didn't have the staples: biscotti, coffee, and sugar. NO MILK. They treated dairy product like poison, although I must make a small confession here: Most of the family, myself included, were lactose-intolerant. However, in deference to all that is sane, I don't believe they even knew what that was.

My cousins and I always lamented the "morning meeting" portion of our schooling because we didn't have the same breakfast eating habits as our peers.

Here's a small sample of what our lives were like in school:

"Good Morning, Class."

"Good Morning Ms. Jones."

"Did everyone eat a good breakfast this morning?"

"Yes, Ms. Jones."

"Who would like to be first to tell what they ate for breakfast?" Little Mary raises her hand, and the teacher nods in her direction.

"I had a poached egg, whole wheat toast, and a glass of milk." The teacher nods in satisfaction.

The next child adds:

"I had a bowl of whole-grain cereal with blueberries on it and a glass of skim milk."

"Oh, isn't that wonderful, boys and girls? Everyone is eating such a nutritious breakfast."

The teacher is quite pleased, and then my cousin MichaelAngelo raises his hand.

"Oh, and what did you have for breakfast this morning, MichaelAngelo?"

"I had a taralle and a biscotti and I washed it down with a cup of black coffee and anisette."

Nice.

But, back to the biscotti. They'd make them with lots of hazelnuts and almonds, and let them dry out so that only horse's teeth could chew through them. Good luck there. Over the years I have tried to perfect my mom's biscotti recipe, and I believe I've done a good job, judging from the raves I receive from everyone who tastes them. They have just the right amount of chewiness, coupled with the right amount of dryness. Really and truly, they are *THE BEST*. Well, everyone says so, and as you've probably realized, these folks never hold back on the truth. I am honored to share this recipe with you:

Italian Biscotti (courtesy of my mom)
Italian name: Quaresimali
Makes approximately thirty biscotti

12 ounces almonds
1 cup flour
2 cups sugar
½ cup light brown sugar
½ cup dark brown sugar
1 teaspoon cinnamon
1 teaspoon baking powder
4 tablespoon softened unsalted butter
3 large beaten eggs

Toast almonds @ 375 degrees for 10 minutes and let cool.

Grind ¼ of the almonds with ¼ cup of sugar.

In a large bowl stir the flour, sugars, cinnamon, and baking powder.

Add butter until combined.

Chop remaining almonds coarsely and add to bowl.

Stir in flour mixture along with eggs and knead until combined. (The dough will be sticky, so wet your hands with water beforehand to handle better).

Divide dough into 2 long rectangles about 3-4 inches across on a cookie sheet lined with parchment paper.

Brush with egg wash (1 egg + 2 tablespoons milk).

Bake at 375 degrees for 25-30 minutes or until browned.

After baking, cool.

Peel off parchment and cut into slices on an angle.

Place cut cookies back on cookie tray and let sit in "Off" oven for 20 minutes. This will give them that extra crunch.

Chapter 8: Fruitcake for the Starving Deer (Dad's "Taste")

Things that made absolutely no sense to anyone made perfect sense to the family. They were sensibly senseless, if that makes any sense! Their ideas were so skewed in one direction that whenever one of them said something was true, the rest would nod in agreement. No matter what it was. They would have what we cousins called "secret covens," where they'd get together in one of the bedrooms, shut the door, and not emerge for hours. When they finally did emerge from their little meeting, they would act like they had been hypnotized, or something. Then they would call out, asking if anyone wanted a cup of tea. Quite frankly, they did love their tea as much as their coffee, particularly Red Rose tea.

Now, it was close to the Christmas holidays one year, and my aunt took out this twelve-pound fruitcake to go with the tea. My dad agreed to have a *taste,* so as not to hurt anyone's feelings (hey, he was an outlaw, oops, sorry, in-law, so he had to behave and eat unpleasant things to keep the peace). My aunt cut him a big-ass piece of fruitcake and put it in front of him. *And he ate all of it.* That was his first mistake. His next faux pas was to actually say, "Oh, B, that fruitcake is delicious." There's your sign. I could have called it—he was plagued with fruitcakes until his dying day. Literally.

My aunt would send Dad a fruitcake through the mail after Thanksgiving, where it would sit in its tin on the dining room floor until the next one arrived a year later, and my mom would throw the old one out into the woods "for the starving deer." The pattern was always the same. Fruitcake arrival after Thanksgiving, one slice eaten, new cake arrives a year later, old one gets chucked out for the deer. Scenario: predictable.

So it came as no surprise that my sister and I actually missed this ritual after my dad died. My aunt stopped sending fruitcakes because, in her words, "Nick loved his fruitcake and now he's gone." That was another of the auntisms. They would say your name, followed by what you liked to eat, as if the food was only for that particular person. Example: "Tes loved her gum," "Nick loved his fruitcake," "Tony loved his macaroni," and so on. If you had expressed joy upon having eaten something as little as ONCE, it became your signature food. (See the chapter on Coconut Custard Pie.)

But back to the fruitcake. My sister decided to make one for Christmas, and since she used up the rest of my Bermuda rum to soak it with, I feel it is a little bit my recipe, too, and I will share it with you:

Nick Loved His Fruitcake Recipe
(Dark Fruitcake)

3 cups all-purpose flour
2 teaspoons baking powder
3 teaspoons cinnamon
1 teaspoon salt
½ teaspoon nutmeg
½ teaspoon allspice
½ teaspoon cloves
1 pound candied fruit
8 ounces raisins
8 ounces cherries
8 ounces dates
1 cup slivered almonds
1 cup pecans
½ cup candied pineapple
4 eggs
1 ¾ cup brown sugar
¾ cup unsalted butter (melted and cooled)
1 cup orange juice
¼ cup molasses

Preheat oven to 300 degrees.

Grease 9-cup Bundt pan or tube pan.

Beat eggs until foamy; add orange juice, butter, and molasses.

Add fruit and nuts.

Combine with dry ingredients and mix well.

Pour into pan and fill no higher than ¾ full.

Bake for 1½ – 2 hours, depending on pan size (some tube/bundt pans are taller than others).

Remove from the oven; invert the pan onto a wire rack and let sit for ten minutes before removing pan. Let cake cool for at least one hour. After one hour, wrap with a rum-soaked cheese cloth (Goslings dark rum is the best, but Bacardi will do), cover with foil and store in refrigerator.

Now, here's where I come in with my two cents: I recommend that every day you take it out and add rum to the cheesecloth, re-wrap, and return to the fridge. Believe me, the liquored-up fools will think they died and went to rum heaven.

Chapter 9: I've Had to Pee Since Paramus

Italian comedians invariably describe American Thanksgiving in an Italian family with the opening line: "First we had the antipasti..."

Predictably, everyone laughs, while the Italian audience all nod knowingly to one another. To be frank about it, the stories are understated.

My Jersey crowd *lived* for Thanksgiving, when they could come to the country, aka *upstate*. Now forget, if you will, the word mob as it's historically been used to describe members of the Mafia. Instead, consider Merriam-Webster's dictionary definition of mob as: "a rowdy, excited crowd." That's more like it. They ought to put surveillance cameras in the homes and cars of these jokers, because their pictures should appear in the dictionary next to the word. How else to describe their group apoplexy at the sight of my parents' house as they neared the driveway?

The cars (yes, cars, plural) would barely have a chance to slow to a stop before the mob would begin to get out. I should say *spill out* because they were crammed in like strett come sardine (packed sardines, to you) so they and the countless items they brought (see chapter 2) would be able to fit.

In the chapter titled "My Big, Fat, Dysfunctional Wedding," I will tell you the story of when they rented a bus, but that's for later.

We had a dirt driveway—what else would you have upstate? So it wasn't until Uncle Joe's brand-new big-ass Cadillac and Uncle Herbie's big-ass Cutlass came to a stop and the dust settled that you could actually see who showed up for the party, unfailingly laden with the goodies that upstate *just didn't have* (or so they were convinced). One time Aunt Marie actually arrived holding in her lap a frozen side of beef because, after, all, one would never be able to buy that in upstate New York.

To make it even crazier, they all talked at once. Imagine the following as one tsunami of sound, thundering toward your house:

"I brought the bread."

"My feet are killing me."

"Like you walked here?"

"I've had to pee since Paramus."

"Uncle Herbie got the cake yesterday."

"Last time you forgot the Tasty Cakes."

"I've had to pee since Mahwah."

"Is Mamie coming over today?" (Not likely—she's been dead for ten years.)

"Where's that cat? You know I hate cats."

"Mama had a cat."

"Mama had a dog, remember?"

"You liked her cat."

"Like hell I did."

"Remember the time…"

"I'm going to pee first thing I get in the house!"

This was my clan at its best, in the middle of constant turmoil and drama.

To this day I never question my parents' motives for moving us upstate.

And so the feasting would begin. Antipasti, stuffed shells with tomato sauce, meatballs, sausage, and braccioles simmering in it to perfection. After that feast Mom would bring out Thanksgiving dinner—turkey with all the trimmings. My mom always felt that there should be another meat for those who didn't like turkey, so she always made a roast beef with baked potatoes for those who wanted.

Yes, the adults sat in the dining room, and the kids sat in the kitchen. You had to wait until someone died to get a spot at the adult table, and it went by seniority. With thirty-seven first cousins, I didn't get a spot at the adult table until I was forty-five years old!

Now, being seated at the kids' table had advantages and disadvantages. To your advantage was the fact that the drunken fools in the next room weren't keeping track of how much soda and wine were being consumed by anyone, therefore you could have all you wanted of both. Score on that one. The disadvantage, however, was that the big people were hoarding all the food on plates and in bowls on that big table in the dining room, and you had to go and get it yourself if you wanted more.

No one likes turkey stuffing like I do. (My mom made the best, and my sister makes it now, just the way she did.) Fresh roasted chestnuts, sausage, sage... good God, my mouth is watering as I write this! Stuck at the kids' table, I always wanted more, but how to get it? That crazy-assed bunch in the next room wouldn't be able to hear the Voice of God above the din, let alone little me, and the stuffing was in the middle of the table!

I was too shy and quiet to go into the dining room, so guess what? Every freakin' year until I was forty-five years old, I ate only what I had been given. The good news is that now my sister always does Thanksgiving Day, bless her heart. My seat is front and center, so you can bet that my big ass eats as much stuffing as it can, and I always show up the next day for leftovers.

I find turkey overrated, but pair it with stuffing and you've got yourself the best meal of the year.

Here's my sister's turkey stuffing recipe:

Worth the Wait Stuffing

Serves 12 to 14 people with some left over
(but not if I'm around)

½ lb. *freshhhhh* chestnuts
6 stalks celery
1 large white onion
1 pound *freshhhh* breakfast sausage, taken out
    of casing
¼ pound unsalted butter
4 tablespoons virgin olive oil
Small bunch *freshhhh* parsley
2 cloves garlic
2½ pounds unseasoned dried bread crumbs
    (Pepperidge Farm in the bag works the
    best)
8 cups homemade (yeah, right) or store-
    bought chicken broth
Pinch of salt and pepper

Score flat side of chestnuts, (with a sharp paring knife, make a half-inch slit in the shape of a cross), then roast at 400 degrees for 20 minutes. Peel, chop, and set aside.

In a large stock pot, melt unsalted butter and virgin olive oil in pan, add sausage, and cook thoroughly.

Remove sausage and add garlic, celery, parsley.

Add salt and pepper to taste.

Cook until celery is tender and onion is translucent.

Add chopped chestnuts TO celery and mix well.

Remove from heat.

Add dried bread, mix thoroughly and begin to add warmed broth in one-cup increments. Add less liquid if you prefer a drier stuffing, more if you prefer a more moist stuffing. (Side note: *DUH*.)

Turn stuffing into a 9 by 11 buttered casserole, or stuff your turkey with it, if you prefer. If you do not stuff the bird, bake in a 350-degree oven until completely heated through. (Again, side note: If you do stuff the turkey, add popcorn kernels to the stuffing and cook until the ass blows off the turkey! Just kidding...)

(I'll bet you thought this chapter was finished, didn't you? Hell, no!)

Now it's time to clear the dishes from the table and let the men make their necessary adjustments in order to make room to eat more, while the women clean up the slimy grease from the turkey carcass. Nice.

As the womenfolk moved back and forth during this process, I would be getting my coat on to help bring Millie Cake (see chapter 5) across the highway. When we returned, we would find the table laden with a multitude of Italian pastries: roasted chestnuts, a big bowl of unshelled nuts, a bowl of fruit, a big-ass fruitcake (for my dad, of course), Tasty Cakes, and a five-pound box of Fanny Farmer chocolates. The added Millie Cake and cream puffs tipped the scales. The locusts would tear into all of it, washing it all down with coffee and anisette.

They would then proceed to retire to wherever they could pass out. Something to ponder here in retrospect: There was only one bathroom.

At five o'clock, my mother would call out, "Let's have a sandwich before you get on the road." Just as in *The Night of the Living Dead*, you'd see these fools emerging from nowhere, lurching their way slowly into the dining room.

Again into the dining room. Only this time, there would be turkey and roast beef sandwiches piled high on the table, along with leftover antipasti tidbits and tea. Since the fruitcake hadn't been opened at dinner, they would open it, to mark the beginning of the Christmas season. Of course, this ritual had to be toasted with glasses of anisette. Then, after fortifying themselves enough to drive the ninety miles home safely, they would plant garlic-breath kisses on everyone, gather up the whining cousins sleeping on the living room floor in their PJs, and make their way back to Jersey.

All was well with the world (and upstate) once more.

Chapter 10: Steak a la Garden Hose

No one could cook a sirloin like my mom. When my husband first started to court me, he was soon to discover that Jacki's meat was "Paped" until it died a respectable death. Well, he called it "Paped"—that was our last name, *Pape*—but he gave this title to all the meats my mother made, because she would cook it until it was charred, blackened (before that became culinary fashion), rendering it impossible to chew, swallow, or digest. My dad LOVED it that way.

And so she'd take an expensive three-or-four-pound sirloin, bone in for the dog to enjoy later (although the poor creature would look at it and whine), plop it onto the broiling pan and stick it under the broiler, which was in a drawer under the oven.

In a GAS OVEN. ON HIGH BROIL. Two inches from the FLAMES.

Many times this would work, but there were times when it didn't even come close. Like this one particular time. I guess the butcher gave her a cut with quite a bit of fat decorating this Heart Attack Special (remember when we thought fatty rind was a food group?). Well, the grease splattered onto the flames. Before long the flames were licking the edges of the stove. My mom screams for me to open the front door, and she then OPENS THE OVEN for all of Satan's flames to draw breath from the OXYGEN, and proceeds to throw the flame-engulfed steak out the front door, where it sails through the air, skids into the grass and dirt, and lands in the geranium garden.

But wait! There's more. Now she takes the garden hose and, while my sister and I plead with her not to do it, she drags it into the kitchen and HOSES DOWN the PORCELAIN stove. Which immediately cracks.

But wait! There's more. She drags the hose back outside and full-throttles it directly onto the steak. You could hear the sizzle fizzle. She then picks the steak up, hoses off the other side, and brings it back into the kitchen.

And this is what she says:

"Put it under the broiler to heat it up. Your father will never know."

One hour later:

"Great steak, Jacki!"

You cannot make this shit up.

Jacki-free Grilled Steak
Serves 2

A nice large sirloin, fat trimmed
4 garlic cloves, minced
Salt and pepper
Basil (optional)
Salt and pepper both sides of steak.

Rub garlic cloves into the meat and let sit at room temp for 30 minutes.

Sometimes, if I have fresh basil in the garden, I will rub some leaves into the meat before grilling. Gives a nice flavor.

Steak Sauce:

¼ cup soy sauce
¼ cup hoisin sauce

Mix the two sauces together to make a marinade.

Grill both sides of the steak to your liking, continually basting with soy/hoisin sauce.

Serve hot. (No hosing required.)

Chapter 11: Blinding Pork Chops

Okay, so you've got the idea about Paped meat. Pork was no exception, and may actually have been tortured on the way to the plate more than any other meat. My mom lived in fear of trichinosis, although I never heard of anyone *ever* getting it, certainly not upstate. So pork was certainly Paped, and then Paped again for good measure.

Now, I was never a fan of pork. Let's be honest and say that maybe it was the way it had been prepared by Mom, but I could never warm up to it. Unfortunately for me, however, we had pork chops at least once a week. So that day was my contribution to vegetarianism.

Anyway, Mom never marinated anything. Pork chops got breaded and fried, and then put into the oven to cook. That's where the good measure came in, every week, when mom would make her killer pork chops. Or *killed*, whichever way you want to look at it.

"Great pork chops, Jacki," you would hear, said in Dad's appreciative voice.

This went on weekly for years.

Two weeks before I got married, my dad went on a business trip, and Mom invited my soon-to-be-hubby and me over for dinner. What did she serve? C'mon, weekly pork chops! Hey, what can I say? She was a creature of habit.

I didn't want to, but for some reason they looked really good that night, so I ate them. And they were delicious. Cooked to perfection, juices running, slightly pink... PERFECT. And then I did the unthinkable. She always made bone-in pork chops, and the meat is the most succulent nearest the bone. So I foolishly took the pork chop into my greasy hands and tried to snap the bone away from the meat. Instead of snapping it away from me, I snapped inward, causing a bone sliver to go into my eye!

I thought the sliver had come out soon after, but days went by and it was getting worse. It was swollen and closed, and now my wedding was a week away! I simply couldn't be suffering from pork chop blindness that day.

I ended up having the bone removed, and my eye patched, despite my protests that I was THE BRIDE, and needed to have BOTH EYES available on that day. (I did remove the patch for the big event.)

That was the only time Mom's pork chops were edible. After that day she continued for almost another twenty years serving my dad Paped pork chops.

As for me, I began to cook boneless pork, and became quite good at it, trying different recipes, using marinades and sauces, always leaving the meat slightly pink. I became a fan of pork, but my mom's chops will live in infamy.

Here's my recipe for boneless pork.

In No Danger Pork Chops
Serves 6

6 boneless, lean pork chops

Mix together:
2 cloves minced garlic
¼ cup soy sauce
4 tablespoons hoisin sauce

Put the chops in a zip lock bag and pour the mixed ingredients into the bag. Let this sit in the refrigerator all day to marinate.

Place the chops on a hot grill and continue to baste with the marinade until the centers are a little pink.

Take off the grill and place on a platter.

I like to serve this dish with a flavorful rice or cous-cous.

Chapter 12: Never Live it Down Pork Stew

So I'll continue with pork, since it held such an honored place in Mom's freezer.

My mother always worried about a famine. I guess if you had grown up in one house with twelve siblings, their spouses and children during WWII, you would, too. My mother went to the butcher on a weekly basis, whether she needed to or not. There was always, say, about thirty-four to fifty-six pounds of some kind of meat in her freezer at any given time, all wrapped up separately in freezer paper, *unmarked*. Why would anyone want to mark the outside with the name of the inside contents? Is it really that important to know what's in the freezer? Just *feel* it—you can tell.

While hubby and I were building our home, we lived at my parents' house. They spent their winters in Florida, so the only responsibility we had was to feed my teenage brother, who was going to college and living at home. Nice gig he had.

Once a week the parents would call from Florida, mostly to see if my sibling had had a wild party (p.s., he had), and if the house was still standing (it was), and to ask if anyone they knew had died. It never mattered if they had, because, in my dad's words "Can't do anything about it from here."

Well, while my dad wanted to know the answer to those things, Mom just wanted to know if there was enough in the freezer to eat, and if I needed to replenish the meat supply. *Um*, I'm thinking, *not until 2003 would we need to buy meat*, but I'd answer her politely with a yes, and then my dad would get back on the phone and ask when the hell we were moving out. He was all about getting back to the insanity in New York. Florida was way too quiet.

Here's the story of the Never-Live-It-Down Stew.

My mom calling from Florida: "Oh, there's stew meat in the freezer that needs to be cooked. Why don't you make a nice stew for the guys?"

"What does it look like, Mom?"

"Oh, just FEEL it. You can tell. It FEELS like stew meat."

So I felt around the paper-covered packages in the freezer until I found something that resembled cut up pieces of meat, put it on the counter to defrost, and headed off to work.

Upon my return in the evening, the meat had defrosted, and I set out to make the stew. Now, although I was a new bride, I considered myself a decent cook. When I unwrapped the package, the meat looked rather gray, but I figured that freezer burn had set in. It wouldn't kill them to eat it, and so I cut up the veggies, browned the meat, and put it all in the pot to simmer away.

The guys were mortified.

"What the hell is THIS?" my husband choked.

"This tastes like dog food," my brother chimed in, liking the fact that hubby is yelling, and now the little shit has a reason to gang up on me.

"What IS it, Gloria? I cannot seem to place the taste!" Hubby's voice descended into kindness because he knew what response his first comment *wasn't* getting him, and he wanted to make quick amends. Brother simply feigned choking and gagging.

"It's stew, fools," I offered, but truthfully, it really was awful, and even I could not place the taste.

We agreed on Three Guys Pizza, but I never lived this down. Never.

When the parents came home, the story was re-counted with glee by the guys: how I almost poisoned them, how it was the worst meal ever, how they still had the bad taste in their mouths, etc.,etc.

"What did you cook?" Mom asked me.

"Stew."

" I didn't have any stew meat in there, did I?"

"Well, there was this package with cut-up chunks and I assumed it was beef for stew."

"Oh, they were PORK chunks. You can't make stew with that!" Really? No shock, Sherlock.

"Well, what were YOU going to make with it?" I asked Mom.

"Stew."

It's thirty-three years later and I still cannot figure out her answer.

Gloria's Crock Pot Real BEEF Stew
Serves 4 to 6

3 to 4 pounds lean chuck roast cut into one-
    inch cubes
4 large white potatoes, peeled and cut into
    one-inch cubes
6 to 8 carrots, cleaned and cut into one-inch
    pieces
28-ounce can crushed tomatoes
2 cups flour
Pinch of pepper and salt
1 cup beef broth
½ cup any dry red wine
3 dried bay leaves

Mix the pepper into the flour and roll the meat in it. Shake off excess.

Put the meat in the bottom of the crock pot. Then add the potatoes and carrots. Add all of the other ingredients.

Cook on low for 8 to 10 hours.

Serve with a warm, crusty bread.

I guarantee you will not be disappointed.

Chapter 13: Steer-Steak Again?

As previously stated, my mother's side of the family didn't have the market cornered when it came to crazy. My dad's side could hold their own as well. Take, for example, my grandmother, Cracker. (Okay, so they didn't have the market cornered when it came to names, either.) We called her "Gram," and then lengthened it to "Gram Cracker." This, of course, always got us laughing, simpletons that we were. Then the inevitable happened, and she wound up as "Cracker." Anyway, when she was still "Gram-Cracker," she would babysit the four of us, my two siblings, my cousin and I, while the adults went away periodically for... well, whatever.

The main attraction here was *LIVER*. Can you imagine? The cholesterol alone... yikes!!! But during the 60s, the parents thought liver had lots of nutrients and iron, so we ate it once a week. They must have failed health class with flying colors, is all I'm saying.

My brother wouldn't touch the stuff, and my sister would just cry, so it was up to Cuz and me to hold down the fort and make sense of it all. And that's when we came up with the steer-steak story. We told the little kids that it was a steer-steak, and that it was delicious and all of the cowboys ate it on the range (yeah, right). And they ate it up. Literally. We even had an anthem we sang to get into the eating mood: "Steer-steak, steer-steak, we love steer-steak." We were idiots.

Of course my mother had *plenty* of liver in the freezer. (See previous chapter.) Gram thought, I'll just fry it up with onions and bacon, throw in a few potatoes, and there's a nutritious meal for four kids. That was Friday night's dinner, Saturday night's dinner, and no way were we eating it again! By the end of Saturday night, my evil cousin had locked poor old Gram Cracker in the bathroom and made her *promise* that she wouldn't serve it a third night. She promised, but he wouldn't open the door for about three hours! We gave up that anthem for another: "Steer-steak, steer-steak, we hate steer-steak." I told you we were simpletons.

So we got hot dogs instead on Sunday evening (another nutritious meal created by good old Cracker). We also got punished for locking her in the bathroom, but I figure it was worth it, because my mother was so appalled that Gram Cracker would DARE to think of serving her children liver three nights in a row, that we didn't have to eat it for six months! Amen to that. Mom didn't really care for her mother-in-law, so we scored big on that one.

And as far as meals with liver went, I gave up eating it after 10th grade Biology class, where I got way too much information. However, if you're interested, I have added the recipe that my mom used when she made her liver dinner. I think the dusting of flour gives it some body.

Steer-Steak (Liver) with Onions and Bacon
(the best part, as far as I'm concerned)
Serves 3 to 4

½ pound bacon
1 pound liver from the butcher, cut into
    serving pieces
1 large onion, sliced
Salt and pepper

Cook the bacon, and then take out of the pan and drain on paper towels, leaving the drippings in the pan.

Dredge the liver in flour mixed with salt and pepper. Fry in the pan of bacon grease.

Add the sliced onion after cooking the liver for 3 minutes, then turn the liver over and cook for another 3 to 4 minutes.

Take the liver out and serve with the bacon.

If you're feeling up to it, why not cut up some potatoes and fry them up as well?

What the hell. Go for it.

Chapter 14: Necking, Petting, and Coconut Custard Pie

Being the youngest of twelve siblings had its advantages and disadvantages for my mom. Take, for one example, the fact that her parents were so old that they probably didn't care who she was with, or who she *was,* for that matter. As a teen, this was fortuitous. However, even if her parents left her alone, you can bet that the nieces and nephews living in the house while her brothers were fighting in WWII overseas never left her alone. She was closer in age to them than to her own siblings, so she was a free built-in babysitter and playmate for many, my cousin Joe Luzzo being one.

Now, my cousin Joey had a reputation for being a "Momma's boy." Really? I always thought that every Italian male came with that title If Joey wasn't attached to his mother's butt, then he was up my mom's. Every chance he got. In reality, my mom was about sixteen years older than Joey, and so her roles were many—big sister, aunt, playmate and, as I mentioned before, babysitter. He was such a high maintenance child that his parents, my aunt and uncle, needed weekend rest from his weekday antics and tantrums. Weekends were reserved for going out to the movies, or down to the local gin mill for a couple of cold ones. Joey was to stay at home with the sitter.

Mom was dating Dad at the time, so he got the full effect of Joey, who hated Dad, plain and simple. And Dad hated Joey. After all, they both loved my mom, and vied for her attentions. Dad said that he could never get close to scoring on a Saturday night because of Joey, who would sit on the couch between the two of them and gaze at my mom, while periodically throwing eye darts at dad. Whenever dad moved in on Mom, Joey was right there, threatening to tell. His threats consisted of screaming at the top of his lungs until dad backed off. Every Saturday night.

Now, my cousin Joey loved *his* coconut custard pie. That's right, folks, that pie was *his* signature food. The way the family story goes, coconut custard pie was his *life*.

And so, one Saturday night, I guess dad's hormones just couldn't take it anymore, and Joey was promised his own, entire, coconut custard pie for keeping his mouth shut. The story gets vague at this point, after so many years of telling, retelling, and yelling it, but I'm guessing that he got his pie and squealed, too. Just a thought. He was that kind of kid.

Anyway, whenever we have coconut custard pie, Joey's name comes up. Of course it does. We're creatures of habit.

You Can't Always Get What You Want Coconut Custard Pie
Serves 6 to 8

Ingredients for pie shell:
  2 cups all-purpose flour
  1 teaspoon salt
  1 ½ sticks plus 3 tablespoons cold unsalted butter
  4 to 6 tablespoons ice water

Whisk everything in a bowl and then stir with a fork until the butter is incorporated. Do not overwork dough, as it will become tough.

Gather dough into a ball and then wrap in plastic wrap and put into fridge for 1 hour until chilled.

Preheat oven to 375 degrees.

Take out dough and roll until round, to fit into a 10-inch glass pie plate. Place dough in plate and fold over to make a rim. Do not crimp. Line pie shell and edges with foil and bake for 20 minutes, then take out of the oven, remove foil, and prick the bottom and edges with a fork, baking again for 15 minutes. Take out and leave oven ON.

In the meantime, mix together:
  5 large eggs
  ¾ cup sugar
  2 cups WHOLE milk
  ½ cup half-and-half
  1 teaspoon vanilla

¼ teaspoon salt
1 cup sweetened flaked coconut

Mix all of the above ingredients together and pour mixture into baked pie shell. Foil the edges, then bake for 30 to 40 minutes until it's a little jiggly in the center.

Take out of oven and cool completely on rack before refrigerating.

Joey would eat his *just like that* (see the chapter on sweet potatoes), but it's best served with a dollop of whipped cream.

Chapter 15: Aunt Gloria's Chocolate Stop-Short Smiley-Face Cake

My Aunt Gloria was no cook. Buttered bologna sandwiches were a staple in her house, and my cousin liked his with mayonnaise, to boot. They had no sense of taste... in case you couldn't tell.

Is it any wonder, then, that they would literally risk their lives in a raging snowstorm to travel to our house for Christmas Eve? Question: What would *you* rather have? Bologna sandwiches on white bread with butter and mayo, or seven delectable fishes with all the trimmings that someone else skunked up their kitchen to cook? And all your fat ass had to do was to sit down and eat it? No brainer.

My aunt would make her famous chocolate cake as the contribution to the table. I wasn't a fan, but I really didn't care because there were so many other goodies to choose from (*HELLO*: Millie Cake) that her cake was insignificant at best, and besides, it came from a *box mix.*

During the day, one Christmas Eve, the skies turned dark, and the forecast was for a blizzard. Faint snowflakes began to fall around two p.m., when the pilgrimage from across the river began. You can bet that my aunt wasn't going to miss Christmas Eve dinner. With my uncle driving and her holding the chocolate cake on her lap, they set off for our house with my cousin in the back seat. Normally we lived only twenty minutes away from them, but the snow really picked up, the roads were icy and visibility was very poor.

My aunt kept nagging my uncle to drive slower, since the cake was balanced precariously. My cousin, for drama's sake, kept asking "Are we there yet?" He had ADHD before anyone knew what that was. I guess my uncle got tired of them both, because without warning he stopped short.

Brakes squealed and Gloria's face fell. Into the cake. Which was frosted. In a box. An uncovered box.

When she picked her face up off the cake, there was a distinct imprint on it, just like the "Have a Nice Day" yellow smiley faces.

Of course the liquored up fools ate her cake anyway, and Millie Cake, too, but this story was told year after year by my cousin. He LOVED drama.

Smiley-Face Cake by Aunt Gloria
Serves 8

I am certain that she used a Betty Crocker cake mix, and doctored it up, but she did make her own butter cream frosting, so here's the recipe for both:

Ingredients for cake:
> 1 package cooked chocolate pudding mix
> 1 box Betty Crocker Devils Food Cake Mix

Preheat oven to 350 degrees.

Prepare one package of pudding mix as per instructions on the box and blend the dry cake mix into the hot pudding.

Pour into two 8-inch round greased and floured pans and bake until cakes springs back when touched.

Buttercream Frosting:
> One 12-ounce package of semi-sweet
>   chocolate chips
> 4 tablespoons unsalted butter
> 6 tablespoons whole milk
> 2 cups sifted confectioner's sugar

Mix until glossy. If not glossy, add a few drops of hot water.

Frost cake as desired.

Chapter 16: Tupperware March Madness

Cracker, my grandmother on my paternal side, was no cook. Remember, she served us liver two nights in a row and planned on a third before advancing to that healthy hot dog meal. Her favorite foods were the ones that contained every imaginable nitrite and nitrate, with as many unpronounceable ingredients as possible. That's how she rolled.

As she got older (hell, she lived to be over 100), Cracker became forgetful and blind in one eye (not that the "good" eye was any better), so we disconnected her stove after she almost burned the complex down making her yummy turkey tettrazini. We bought her a microwave, and she LOVED the damn thing. It was her gateway to all that was good in the culinary arts: hot dogs, Jimmy Dean sausages, TV dinners. She lived for salt-ridden, nitrite-infested food. If it was micro-wavable, it was dinner. Cracker lived on her own until she was 100, and she would no doubt owe it all to mega-processed foods.

She also believed in the health value of a dry martini with two olives and a piece of cheese every day at four. Additionally, she smoked three packs of Winstons a day until she was 85, when her doctor suggested that she should quit, so she did. You couldn't kill her with a silver bullet.

Cracker was also partial to sausage and peppers for dinner. She'd put it all into a glass pan, and nuke it on high until the sausage popped open. That was her signal that it was done. She would make enough for a few meals, and I guess that at her age the four o'clock martini was enough to fill her up, so she had lots of leftover sausage and peppers . She'd put them into a plastic Tupperware container and then store the container in one of the lower kitchen cabinets. For the next time.

Two weeks after one such meal...

Cracker goes into the cabinet and sees the container and asks herself, "What's this? Wow! It's sausage and peppers. Great! I won't have to blow up sausages in the microwave for tonight's dinner. I'll just eat these."

And she does.

Two hours later, Cracker realizes that the tasty meal she has consumed was in fact left *unrefrigerated for two weeks.*

Her phone call to my aunt:

"Gloria?"

"Yes, Mom" (exasperated tone).

" You need to know that if I die tonight it was because I ate sausage and peppers that had been in the cabinet for two weeks."

"Really?" (hopeful voice).

"Yes."

"Okay, Mom. Good luck!"

My aunt Gloria was like that. Unfailing care and concern.

Unbelievably, Cracker was fine. If that had been one of us, we would have needed our stomachs pumped, *if* we lived long enough.

But that's the way Cracker rolled.

Cracker's Better Days Sausage and Peppers
Serves 3 to 4

Buy the cheapest sausage you can find
Green peppers
One onion

Cut up some green peppers and one onion and throw it all into a glass pan. Nuke it on high until the sausages pop open... then they are done.

Okay, now for a *real* sausage and pepper recipe:
Preheat oven to 375 degrees
> One pound Premio sweet Luganiga sausage
> (it is thin and coiled in the package)
> One red pepper, one green pepper, one yellow
> pepper, cut into chunks
> One sweet Vidalia onion, cut into chunks

Place all ingredients into a roasting pan and cook at 375 degrees for approximately 1 hour and 15 minutes. Serve.

Note: Premio also makes basil and cheese sausage, and a rosemary/herb sausage, and both are delicious. Sometimes it's nice to mix them together as well. I serve this with nice, crusty fressssssh bread and a green salad.

Chapter 17: Chunky Light and Her Jewish Pizza

As college students, we thought we were the shit when it came to cooking, but it turns out that it was our cooking that was shit.

There were ten of us living in squalor in a college town in upstate New York (REAL upstate) and seven of us were Italian. We considered ourselves cooking savants and were sure everyone in the house would salivate when they tasted our food. We should have stuck with the studying.

Since we had friends in the neighboring college town, we reserved Sundays for "family" dinners with them. Each of us would cook our specialty, and mine was meatballs. Now, don't even go there as to why, in the name of all that is holy, I didn't make them the way my aunt did (see chapter 2). But I didn't. Instead, since we had an abundance of oregano from Wegmans (translated, that means $.99 per pound), and we were poor, I used about thirteen ounces in two pounds of ground chuck (also $.99 per pound) for our meatballs. WE. WERE. POOR.

It didn't get better when the others cooked, either. My housemate Arleen cooked a chicken *from a can*. I had never seen such a thing, but she bought it at Wegmans for $1.99. The sucker was WHOLE. She birthed it from the can like a midwife, no joke. I personally couldn't eat it after that scene, but she ate my portion with no trouble. We were poor.

My meatballs were green with oregano, and I threw the last three ounces into the tomato sauce. Nice touch. At Wegmans, spaghetti was four pounds for $.99 (are you seeing a pattern here?) so we made all four pounds for the four of us this one afternoon. Our friends from the neighboring college stopped at a bakery and bought four cannolis. Readers, there is NO place then, now, or EVER that will ever make an edible cannoli to equal the ones here in downstate. Seriously. These looked like turds. But I will get to that.

Our meal was ready. The person in charge of pasta said that the only way to eat it was al dente, but all I heard was "dente," which is how my teeth felt after eating this pasta. You could have caulked the walls with it, that's how al dente it was. I bathed it in sauce and meatballs, we put a little Velveeta on the top (WE WERE POOR) and we sat down to eat. Arleen took the infant out of the oven and we began our descent. We ate like longshoremen.

We polished off about three pounds of pasta and the oregano meatballs. I passed on the chicken. After all, I did have my pride.

It was time for dessert. We used to use and reuse teabags. You know why. We had a little string that was attached to the wall in our kitchen where we'd hang up our teabags to be reused. The water was put on the stove for reusable tea, and we cleaned up and took the cannolis out of the fridge and placed them on the table. I mentioned before what they looked like, but we dove in anyway. Yup, it was confirmed.

I don't believe that ANY of us eating this slop that day thought it was great, but we kept on eating. Maybe because we didn't want to admit defeat, or maybe our circumstances dictated that we needed a meal. In any case, it would take five years into the future for us to realize how stupid we were when it came to cooking.

Chunky Light was one of our housemates. She was from a town where the big event was the fire truck being washed and polished once a week. I am not joking. She wasn't Italian. I'm not even sure she *had* a nationality. In any case, she ate tuna fish like it was her job. Every day. She'd open a can and proceed to make it three different ways, one for each meal. For example, breakfast was straight up tuna to get the blood flowing. The lunch portion was made with miracle whip, and she'd set aside the third portion to be made at dinner. That was what we called Jewish Pizza. I'll give you that recipe at the end of this chapter.

Consequently, our house smelled like the Bumblebee factory in Astoria, Oregon, which was not OK. We'd had enough of the gross smells emitting form our kitchen. We'd had a basement flood earlier in the year and I leave it to you to imagine why. We were DONE with smells. So we decided to hold our own version of an intervention.

This intervention involved a can of chunky light

tuna (courtesy of Wegmans), a can of Little Friskies tuna-flavored cat food (also courtesy of Wegmans), and nine sorority sisters. We steamed the labels off the cans and switched them. We then put the "tuna" can in the pantry and waited for it to happen.

It didn't take long for—goodness, I cannot even remember her real name—to start searching for a little something for dinner. She was on the larger side, and the tuna was her way of dieting. Without missing a beat, she took out the can of "tuna" and opened it with the rusty manual can opener we possessed. We were absolutely apoplectic with glee as we watched her dump the can into a bowl and mix it with Miracle Whip. As we held our breath and watched, she suddenly stopped and sniffed the bowl, then looked up to ask us, "What's up with the chunky light?"

She never did eat the cat food, but we laughed about it for weeks afterward. The name "Chunky Light" stayed with her until graduation, when we went our separate ways. I will tell you this: She always looked carefully before she opened another can. As for us, we adopted and adapted her Jewish Pizza recipe. It was a great dinner, and cheap, too. We were all about saving money in those days. WE. WERE. POOR.

Jewish Pizza
Serves 1 to 2

1 package English Muffins (we always bought Wegman's brand, but you can use another brand if you like)
1 can tuna fish packed in oil (I'm not going there...)
1 package sliced Velveeta cheese (*absolutely must* be Kraft Velveeta brand)

Pre-heat oven to broil
Make your tuna the way you like it. We always made it with mayonnaise.
Toast 2 English muffins.
Spread the English muffins with tuna fish.
Put a slice of Velveeta on top of each muffin.
Place under the broiler until cheese melts.
Eat.

I don't know why it got the name Jewish Pizza, but in upstate New York, that's what they called it.

Chapter 18: There's a Squirrel in the Crock Pot

I've spent a lot of time talking about my crazy family escapades in the kitchen, but I haven't mentioned the ex-brother-in-law's escapades (he's deceased), so now is a good time to get that story over with.

"Wicked Will," as we called him, was a gun-toting, beer-drinking, euphemism-throwing kind of guy. His favorite "Wicked-ism" was "F@#%'m if they can't take a joke."

Believe me, no one thought he was ever joking. Once, in a real old-fashioned Currier and Ives Christmas moment, he flashed twenty unsuspecting carolers as they belted out "Deck the Halls." I guess in his drunken stupor he heard "Halls" with a "B," and came out to greet them as the main event. You can bet that bunch didn't stay for the cookies and hot chocolate. My sister yanked him back into the house, kicking and screaming out his favorite "Wicked-ism."

The "Deck the Balls" incident was just one of many, such as when my Mom cooked squid in the tomato sauce one Christmas Eve. Wicked Will plucked one out of the pot and ran around the house to show the little kids what he found in the sauce. The kids screamed as he chased them around and around until my sister yanked Will upstairs and put *him* to bed. Yup, you guessed it. His final message before going off into a booze slumber was his favorite Wicked-ism.

Anyway, one of his activities, when he wasn't terrorizing the neighborhood, was hunting both large and small game. He came from a family of professionals, and they all hunted. They had a camp in upstate NY where they kept their hunting gear year round. But Wicked Will liked to hunt locally, *really locally*, aka the backyard.

Nothing was safe from his bullets or his crock pot. Once, during the winter before I got married, we were snowed in for three days. Even if the stores had been open, which they weren't, we wouldn't have been able to get to them. People were bunkered in and camped out, wherever there were homes with heat. Most everyone was without power, and in my neighborhood most everyone had at least a gas stove or a wood stove.

Wicked Will had a generator for such emergencies (of course he did) so the logical place to camp out was his house. Wicked was all about the "camping" aspect of this ordeal. Nothing was too good for the in-laws. He shared his Budweiser and Seagrams with all of us. It was a *PARTY.* Even his mother showed up, and she was all about the Bud.

"Get me a cold one, will ya?"

"You betcha, Ma."

He was endeared to his mother. They liked the same things.

On the third day of this soiree, my mom, sister, and I couldn't decide what to cook. Cabin fever was setting in, although the electric company was promising relief within twenty-four hours. Hearing this, and knowing that the party would soon be over, Wicked got an idea.

"Hey, we've got some meat left over from camp in the freezer, and I'm going to make all of you squirrel stew."

Now of course we didn't believe him, because he had been nursing a bottle of Seagrams all afternoon, so we figured the booze was doing the talking.

At this point Wicked took a freezer-wrapped parcel out of the fridge (remember, he had a generator), and then proceeded to produce carrots, celery, potatoes, onions, and spices. We were laughing, because we figured the package was a pot roast of some sort. He threw everything into the crock pot, turned it on, and went back to Seagrams and gin rummy with Ma.

The rest of us went outside to shovel ourselves out.

6 p.m.

"Dinner's ready!" Ma shouted from the front door, which, I might add, only opened thanks to my shoveling all afternoon. I didn't care. I was getting drunk from second-hand booze every time they opened their mouths. It felt good to be outside and away from the booze and kitchen smells. Whatever was in the crock pot stank up the house. It smelled like... a dead animal in the woods.

As we all sat down to eat, Wicked put a serving dish on the table. In the middle of the dish there were two large hunks of meat surrounded by the potatoes and vegetables. The hunks faintly resembled, well, squirrels. Without the heads, of course.

"C'mon, dig in," said Wicked.

Ma filled her plate by tearing through a piece of meat with her fork, first stabbing it and raking it downward until she pulled a piece off. She licked her fork, made the yummy sound, and dove back in to stab a few potatoes and carrots, while my parents and I looked on in disgust and disbelief.

"C'mon, get it while it's hot," said Wicked gleefully, as he followed Ma into the dish, the two of them digging into their food like it's the Last Supper. Meanwhile, I gingerly reached in with my fork and knife to cut off a tiny piece of whatever it was, and to retrieve a potato.

When I finally gathered up the courage to taste what was on my fork, I found out it wasn't as bad as I thought. But it was the only piece I ate.

All this time, Wicked was beside himself with happiness. "Gotcha!" he cried out.

"What do you mean? These aren't really squirrels?" I asked, feeling a tad better already.

"They're squirrels all right, but they ain't from camp. They're local. I shot 'em in the backyard."

Wicked's now puffed up like a proud peacock. What a guy.

Suffice it to say, they really were squirrels, and I really did eat them. Okay, I had a little piece, enough to be able to add squirrel to the repertoire of my life's unusual eats.

I will never be able to tell you that it tasted like chicken, because it didn't. It tasted like *squirrel*.

What can I say?

Crock Pot Squirrel Stew
Serves 4 to 6

2 skinned and cleaned (you know what *that* means) gray squirrels
3 pounds peeled potatoes
1 onion, cut into chunks
6 carrots, cleaned, peeled and cut up into chunks
Salt and pepper to taste
Bay leaves
1 can beef broth

Place all ingredients into the crock pot and set to low for 6 hours.
Take out of crock pot and place on a platter.
Serve.

Chapter 19: The Come-Back-to-Life-Fish and Snakes for Dinner

Apparently, when my great grandparents were alive they felt the need to eat eels on Christmas Eve. This was among many other crazy things, like the baccala. Baccala, or cod, as it is more widely known, which was purchased at the fish market, already dried to look like the papyrus the ancient Egyptians wrote on, then taken home and soaked in salt water to make it soft and plump again. Now how ridiculous is that? Why go through all of that trouble when you could have bought it *freshhhhh* in the first place?

And the stench! Good God, they'd have it soaking in a tub in the kitchen for a week! Yummy! Sign me up now! Cannot wait!

Anyway, this story is about the other "white meat" they ate. The EEL.

Now, I am going under the assumption that the Hudson River was at one time a place where you could actually eat what you fished. There might have been all types of edible fish in the Hudson, so why the hell would anyone think it was okay to eat a *snake*? My great-grandparents did. So much so that in their eyes it wasn't Christmas Eve without both the freeze-dried, soaked, come-back-to-life fish *and* the eels.

At that time eels could be purchased from the fish market, not the snake charmer down the street, so my mother brought it home in a bag, *alive* on Christmas Eve. (I was not charmed.) Then she'd kill it (I'm not so sure how, but I think it involved whacking off the head with one quick motion), and put it in a pan. She would put salt and pepper on it and stick it in the oven for I do not know how long.

When it debuted from the oven, the top skin of the eel would be crisp, but no one ate that part. Mom would then make cuts into the body, leaving it like that in the pan, and then she'd present it to the table. You can call it anything you like, but to us it was a *snake*. I was old enough to remember this, but too young to remember if I was upset by it or not.

When I was growing up, my dad always took me fishing on the river, and the only things I ever caught were eels. I hated the way they squirmed on the line, the hook in their snakey mouths, writhing and trying to get free. Dad, like all good catch-and-release-fishermen, would take them off of the hook and return them to the depths of the Hudson. Best part of fishing, as far as I was concerned.

Even now I will not fish in the Hudson, because I know that eels will be all I'll catch. While the rest of the anglers catch bass, sturgeon, catfish, and so on, I will catch EELS. And this chick is not the least bit interested. The first Christmas after the old-timers were gone to rest, Mom breathed a sigh of relief when she realized that eels would no longer be needed at the groaning board.

Amen, I say to that.

Snakes on a Plate (or Baked Eel)
Serves 8 to 10

Two pounds eel, skinned, cleaned, and split
¼ cup flour with salt and pepper mixed in
¼ cup unsalted butter

Preheat oven to 400 degrees and butter a baking dish.

Dredge the eel in the flour mixture and place in pan.

Dot with unsalted butter and add a little water to prevent burning.

Cover and bake for 15 minutes until browned.

Place on a long serving platter and cut into two-inch chunks.

Chapter 20: Get the Lead Out Easter Pies

Food is the great equalizer when it come to tradition, family, and holidays. I do not think there is any ethnic group that doesn't have its share of cooking stories and wonderful recipes to accompany them.

The highest Holy Days in the Catholic faith are those during and after the Lenten season. Lent marks the beginning of fasting until Holy Saturday, and in some Italian households we wait until noon on that day to break the fast, as we had to when the great-grandparents were alive.

And then the cooking and feasting begin.

These days we cook our fast-breaking Easter food on Palm Sunday. There are a lot of traditions that died with the elders, many with good reason. In our world today we all work and we're all busy, yet so many of us still desire to continue traditions. Adapting these old traditions enables us to do both.

That same mother of mine who "Paped" food also made Leaded Easter Pies. You really could have used them for anchors, especially since she stuffed them with so much ricotta that they invariably would *burst open in the oven*, causing the fire alarm to scream whenever it was hit by the smoke they created. The hot cheese would melt under the pies, causing them to blacken underneath. Using a spatula to look, mom would deem them ready to come out of the oven when the bottoms were black, even though the insides would be barely cooked. She liked cooking much of her food this way, blackened on the outside, raw on the inside.

Similarly, Mom would boil her tomato sauce for five minutes, and then turn the stove off. Her sauce never simmered for hours, as it should have, and consequently Tums became a favorite after dinner mint. My husband referred to her tomato sauce as "red lead" because it gave him heartburn for three days after eating it. He never told her though; outlaws learn to keep their mouths shut (well, except yours truly).

However, my husband always knew enough never to go *near* her Easter Pies at all. He said he couldn't. The one attempt he made early in our marriage caused me to think I was going to be a young widow, that's how much pain he was in. So he always made an excuse, or he took a piece that ended up eaten by the kids or the dog. I'll give him one thing: He was quick to learn.

Another term for a Leaded Easter Pie would be a calzone on steroids. Get a load of Ma's list of light and airy ingredients: pot cheese, fresssssssh ricotta and mozzarella, baked ham, pepperoni, sweet and hot sausage, parmesan cheese, and about five dozen eggs to go into both the dough and the filling.

On Palm Sunday morning, the cooking would commence. First, she'd make the leaded dough that would sit in your stomach till the Fourth of July. Then she'd get an obnoxiously large bowl, the size you'd give a baby a bath in, and in it she'd mix up the filling while the dough raised, as much as lead ever can.

She would then take every cookie sheet we owned and on them she'd construct these super-sized calzone-like Easter pies, filling the stretched-out dough and folding it over. Then she'd crimp the edges, brush egg wash all over them, and pop them into the oven. (Well, *pop*'s not exactly the word for such heavy lifting. *Plunk*, maybe.)

Whatever was left over, and it would be a lot, she would make everyone take home, wrapped in folds of aluminum foil. We all took home plenty. "I'll go over, but I'm not eating any pies," my husband would say each year, echoed by the kids. Those who ate them *still* went home with a big-ass Easter pie, along with a belly-ache worthy of a Coney Island all-you-can-eat contest.

When mom passed and we went through her kitchen gadgets, we found the Easter Pie recipe on a yellowed envelope. (We also found some very scary gadgets we began playing around with, but, back to the pies.) My brother asked if he could have the pie recipe, and my sister and I were totally okay with that, because we couldn't imagine eating those again. Meanwhile, the nosy neighbors were peeking through the windows during her kitchen cleanout, trying to see what we were going to leave behind.

We did find about 300 packets of jellies from diners across America. Apparently mom thought diners and restaurants put them out on the table for people to take home, since you never know when having them might just come in handy. You know, in the event of a jelly famine. *It could happen.* And we also noticed that she took care of any possible Splenda and Equal famines, as well.

So, a few years later, my brother finds the Easter pie recipe in his garage in a pile of kitchen gadgets that he was really serious about keeping in the family—meat tenderizer, cheese grater, potato peeler, all, rusty from the humidity. Let's pass those down to the next generation. Hell, put them into the Will, too. I know my kids will fight over them.

Although my brother was reluctant to pitch the Smithsonian kitchen gadgets, he was rather serious about giving the Leaded Easter Pies a whirl. When I informed my husband of Tom's plan, he reminded me, "I don't do Easter Pies," so of course I had to reply, "You don't 'do' much of anything." Ha,ha. Now he was pissed off, and said "You know how sick I get from that stuff?" Well, he didn't say *stuff.* I said, "Tom is making the effort to keep the tradition alive for the kids. The least you can do is go over and show some support."

Translated, this is me saying, "I've had to eat three-bean salad, diarrhea lasagna (do NOT ask) and diet root beer at your family's house, so you'd better buck up and go." I was all about his being diplomatic, to keep my family peace. The words *diplomatic* and *in-laws,* used in the same sentence when talking about his family is the definition of oxymoron, in my book.

Come Palm Sunday, and off we went. My brother had invited several unsuspecting friends of his, and I worried that once they ate this stuff, he wouldn't have any more friends. Either they'd keel over with stomach cramps, or they would never speak to him again, largely because they would all be dead.

My sister-in-law had put out olives and a green salad (bless her), and I start to realize that the salad isn't big enough for everyone to eat as a main course, that I'd better take my portion first. As I do, the first Leaded Easter Pie comes out of the oven. This one has meat in it, though Tom's made a few with spinach and broccoli for the vegetarians.

Admittedly, the smell is intoxicating. (Yeah, so were Mom's. But you can't tell the important things about food until it settles in the lower intestine.) Tom lets it sit for a few minutes, and then begins to cut slices. Everyone grabs. I push hubby to the front of the line. I want to make sure he suffers, since I got myself all lathered up, just thinking about his family.

"Ooh."

"Ahhhh."

"OMG!"

"It's *wonderful...*"

This bunch of moochers sounds like the first ten minutes of a porn film, the way they are carrying on. They've got me now. I'm curious, so I take a slice. I cut a piece with my fork and bring it to my lips. How much damage can one bite do? As it goes into my mouth and I actually *taste* it... I find it to be heavenly.

These were, hands down, no exaggeration, *The. Best. Easter. Pies. EVER.* So light and airy, browned to perfection, with a filling like air... they really could have floated, that's how light they were. I finished the first piece and went on to have another and, I do believe, *another*. Of course little bro' is beaming like he's discovered America, and all of his guests are impressed.

Tom says he followed Mom's recipe, but I think he may have done something more, like *actually let the dough rise*. I think that's the step she didn't do. Mom was always in a hurry.

Anyway, thanks to Tom we have been blessed with the real deal for several years now, and no one ever says no to eating or taking home Easter Pies any more. Some even put in special requests for vegetables or extra cheese. I always say, put a pork chop in the window, and they will come. Hungry and empty-handed. That's the way moochers roll.

Here's our family recipe, courtesy of Mom and Tom, as written in my mom's hand on an old envelope:

The Real Deal Easter Pies
This yields 6 to 8 pies, which should serve 12

Dough ingredients:
    15 cups flour
    6 packages active dry yeast
    6 cups water
    6 tablespoons sugar
    6 tablespoons salt
    6 tablespoons Crisco shortening
    8 extra large eggs (I add a few more, maybe 2
        to 3—they make the dough light)
    One egg plus 2 tablespoons whole milk (for
        egg wash)

In a large bowl, mix all ingredients thoroughly and
knead really well for about 10 minutes.
    Cover the bowl with plastic wrap and set to rise in
a warm, dry place.

Filling:
    5 pounds *freshhhh* whole milk ricotta
    3 pounds shredded whole milk mozzarella
    10 extra large eggs
    5 pounds cooked sweet Italian sausage, casing
        removed
    2 pounds ham, cooked and cubed
    1 pound pepperoni, cubed
    Salt and pepper

Preheat oven to 375 degrees.

Mix all ingredients into a big bowl.

When the dough has risen sufficiently, break off small amounts and stretch to make a round pizza-size shape, approximately 12 inches round.

Fill the middle with the filling and then fold the circle in half, pinching the sides closed.

Brush the top with an egg wash of one egg + 2 tablespoons milk.

Bake until golden, usually 30 minutes, oven depending

Slice, eat, and enjoy hot or cold.

Chapter 21: Fried Oreos Make Happy Campers

Here's a sure-fire way to bond with friends and family:

Buy a camper for $30,000 and a $35,000 Dodge Ram to tow it, so that instead of staying in your $500,000 mortgaged home with central air, and sleeping on 600-count sheets on a king-sized mattress in a room that has a 56-inch plasma TV screen and Movies on Demand, you can drive 100 miles north and *camp.* Sounds like a plan, doesn't it?

I never could understand the theory behind this type of camping. I mean, why? The only time camping should be an acceptable practice is if you are a scout and you need to earn "THE CAMPING" badge. To me, a night at the Super8 is as close to camping as I'll ever want to be.

My brother's family and their many friends all had campers, homes on wheels with all of the amenities. When they "camped" they brought the satellite dish along so they wouldn't miss the Nascar races. They made sure they lacked for nothing, so they brought it all with them. Judging from what I witnessed in the campgrounds we visited, so did everyone else.

Now, camping has its own set of food rules. Hot dogs and burgers are only for lunch or dinner for the kids. I like to refer to camping cuisine as the "Artery Attack." This bunch couldn't wait to go camping for a week, just to eat, well, things no one should be seen eating.

"I'm bringing all the fixins' for homemade egg rolls."

"Yeah, we'll throw them in the turkey fryer."

"Sweet! I'll go to Gander Mountain and buy ten gallons of peanut oil. You think that's enough?"

"Well, I'm making the Bisquick-coated chicken wings with the buttered hot sauce. They take a lot of oil."

"Don't forget, we'll be frying up those ribs, too,"

"And the Oreo cookies. We'll need more Bisquick batter to dip those."

"Maybe we should get another ten gallons, just in case. We can always take it home."

And then my brother says:

"I'm doing a lamb."

There's complete silence. The teenagers are utterly freaked out and one says "*BAAAAAAAD* Uncle Tom."

With all of this there's been not one mention of steamed or broiled *anything*. In fact there's a moment when someone says, "Hey! Why don't we batter and fry all the vegetables too?"

Hell, why not? Why not fry the car?

The pilgrimage to the campsite looks like a wagon train laden with kids, teens, and the artery attack groceries. Not to mention the twenty-five cases of beer to

110

wash it down, plus bicycles, canoes, skateboards, boogie boards, and a few dogs in tow. Simple country fun.

At the campsite, the only things to do are sit, drink, and wait for the next meal. Some of the campers are sporting Bounce dryer sheets on their legs and arms, as well as wearing them Rambo-style around their heads. This year is a bad one for mosquitoes, and the management is handing out Bounce sheets to all who haven't yet been carried away by the biting bugs. They assure us that Bounce dryer sheets will keep the biting insects at bay. *NOT.*

A typical day begins like this:

7 a.m. Someone crawls out of a camper and begins to fry up nine pounds of bacon, then toasts three loaves of bread in bacon grease. YUM. Adding some butter to the pan, he or she scrambles two-and-a-half-dozen eggs. There are only seven of us for breakfast, so they are going light on the food this morning.

8:30 a.m. All are assembled around two picnic tables, eating fried bacon, toast, and eggs, washing it down with Bud Light with Seagrams chasers. Afterward, they move to their lawn chairs, where they sit around until noon. Everyone is now wearing dryer sheet couture.

Noon. "Anyone feel like a hot dog or something?"

No one answers. They are all passed out. Drunk. Trying to forget about the mosquitoes. And the dryer sheets.

5 p.m. Someone fires up the turkey fryer, and there's some stirring from the lawn chairs. One family says they've had enough and they pack up. Which is to say they just throw everything into the cab of their truck and pull away from the site. We wave goodbye, which also doubles as swatting mosquitoes.

5:30 p.m. The woman responsible for the Bisquick fried chicken begins to dunk raw chicken pieces into a batter she's made. Her husband puts them into the 500 degree peanut oil and they sizzle like an egg on a rooftop in July. He quickly takes them out, and wife rolls them into a butter-and-hot-sauce mixture. The crowd has awakened, running to the fryer and back as fast as they can, carrying their food into the netted tent. The mosquitoes are gaining on them.

6 p.m. The next couple begins to dip Oreo cookies into what's left of the chicken batter. I'm thinking that this can't be safe food handling, but we're all delirious from the toxic meld of Bounce, frying oil, and the mosquito bites.

6:30 p.m. The same crowd runs from the shelter of the mosquito tent toward the fryer, where molten, fried Oreos are offered on a dripping slotted spoon. The simple country crowd takes a break from roughing it to grab the Oreos and run back into the safety net.

9 p.m. Groaning with indigestion, the campers make their way into their homes on wheels one by one, pausing only to say goodnight. Hubby and I are sharing a tent, and we turn in, hoping for the best.

6 a.m. I get up after a night of tossing like salad in a bowl. Hubby and I have been sharing an aerobed that turns into a trampoline every time he moves his fresh-from-the-fryer backside. But somewhere during the night the bed lost air and my face got impaled on a rock underneath the tent floor. I make my way out of the tent, hunched over, every bone sore and having a very bad hair day, and I see my brother and my nephew at the fire pit. Apparently it's their turn to make another healthy breakfast. Just as I open my mouth to say good morning, an explosive, teeth-rattling, ground-shaking fart rocks our tent, billowing the sides outward, then sucking them in.

Hubby has awakened.

And this is why I do not camp. Ever.

Better Batter Fried Chicken

You will have to decide how much chicken you want to cook, and then make the batter accordingly:

Serves 4

One chicken, cut up, skin on and bone in
One cup buttermilk
2 cups Bisquick
Peanut oil

Pre heat a deep fryer to 450 degrees

Dip the chicken pieces into the buttermilk, then dredge in the Bisquick.

Place in refrigerator for several hours.

Take chicken out of refrigerator, dip *again* into the buttermilk and dredge *again* in the Bisquick.

Fry in deep fryer in peanut oil and drain onto paper towels.

Hot sauce ingredients:
½ cup melted salted butter
½ cup *red hot* hot sauce

Mix together and dip your chicken in it.

Clams in the Honey Pot

While I am still on the subject of camping and cooking, let me tell you about another inspiring event from the rustic world of the campground.

One summer the trip to our favorite campground found everyone in a not-so favorite camping spot. It seems that the gang decided too late in the season to rent space, and they all ended up on the undesirable far side of the lake.

Hubby and I arrived mid-week. (Remember, I gave up camping, so we're only staying until the s'mores are finished, and then going to the Super8.

Our feet began sinking into the ground the moment we stepped out of our truck.

"Did you guys get rain up here?"

"Nope."

"What's up with the soaking wet ground?"

Silence.

"Did you have the water balloon fight already?"

Silence.

Okay, we give up asking and begin drinking.

After about an hour, we realize that the fryer-chicken-dunking woman's husband is not around.

"Hey, where's Frank?"

"Oh, Cathy had a woolie for steamed clams, so she sent Frank out to get them early this morning and he isn't back yet."

No shit, he isn't back yet. We are *in the Adirondacks* for crying out loud. Where the hell was he going to find clams?

Whatever. We continue drinking.

Around supper time that evening, Frank pulls up in his car, jumps out and says

"Hey guys! Look! I got a bushel of clams!"

As he takes the bushel out of the back seat to show us, the entire bushel spills out onto...

The wet ground.

Everyone is beyond themselves with grief. I cannot even begin to recount the behavior of these drunken fools as they first sound genuinely upset, then begin to laugh hysterically.

I figure there's a joke I missed here somewhere, so I ask again, only this time I *think* I know the answer. Again. "Why is the ground soaking wet?"

"Because you're standing in the honey pot!"

Only now it's worse. Tonight's dinner is *in* the honey pot.

Frank is not worried.

"Hey guys, I'm going to steam them. Don't worry."

Yeah Frank, I'm not worried because I saw an *Applebees* right next to the Super8, and that's where my fat ass is going for dinner.

Frank gets the water in the all-purpose fryer to boil, and drops the clams in. He's spooning them out with a large slotted spoon as they open, but funny, no one's eating them.

"Guys, they're okay to eat, really. C'mon, I drove seven-and-a-half hours to get these suckers. Look, I'm eating them, they're great."

Have you ever had the Asian Chicken Salad at Applebees? *Delicious.*

Chapter 22: Cocktail Sauce and Communion Suits

If funerals were their excuse to fry veal cutlets, certainly this bunch loved a family reunion as much as any trip to the funeral home.

When the aunts and uncles were all alive, reunions would take place at one of their houses, including my parents'. Of course, these gatherings were not to be confused with trips upstate, holidays, weddings, or funerals. The reunion was reserved for just that: a reunion

In 1977, before I had my big, fat, dysfunctional wedding (stayed tuned, that chapter is coming up), my cousins Josephine and Mikey-boy, not to be confused with one of the other fifteen Michaels in the family, had an end-of-summer reunion. And they did the unthinkable: They called it a "cousins' reunion." The aunts went buck wild with that one, and Aunt Santa took to her bed in despair for a week before it was resolved that EVERYONE could attend—aunts, uncles, cousins, long-lost relatives, significant others, everybody. I suppose the aunts all thought we couldn't do without them, or their food.

Josephine and Mikey-boy lived in a ritzy part of Jersey called "The Lake." Mikey-boy was a "contractor," so he had his house custom built, right down to the throne in the powder room. It was embedded with beach glass that had been imported from the coast of New Zealand. When we toured their home and we got to this room, all I could think of were naked pygmies bending over, collecting glass from a sweltering beach. I laughed at my vision, and got the back of my head slapped by an aunt. Crazy. On both counts.

Anyway, these cousins didn't "do" cooking. Everything was catered from several places, so as to get the best of everything. We had mussels in marinara sauce, stuffed clams oreganato, shrimp with a cocktail sauce, king crab legs, lobster tails, and crispy calamari from the fish market. A tenderloin of beef, pork medallions, chicken francese, chicken marsala, chicken cutlets, chicken parmesan, and a honey ham from the butcher made up the meats. Other delectables were salads, pastas, olives, bread, bread, and more bread, and antipasti trays from the local deli. Did I mention that we also had bread?

Every kind of pastry, cake, cookie, and candy was tastefully arranged on the sideboard in the dining room. All of these came from the local pastry shop. Both the pastry shop owner and the deli owner must have owed Mikey-boy a BIG favor, because there was enough food to feed everyone in Jersey.

The aunts, who all insisted on *bringing their own homemade food* to this feast, were appalled when they got there. *They* had *never* called a caterer in their lives. Despite protests that there would be enough, they brought anyway. Sauce and meatballs, fried veal cutlets, sausage and peppers, roast beef, salads—all of it. My cousin Josephine graciously allowed them to fill her kitchen with their dishes, but really, everyone was happy with the catered stuff. It was different, and we enjoyed it.

In retrospect, I think the aunts couldn't bear the thought of the younger crowd gossiping without their input. They were like that, nosy. And they sure had a lot to be nosy about.

Jo and Mikey-boy had this big-assed in-ground swimming pool in the landscaped backyard, resplendent with patio, lounge chairs, built-in grill, cabana, and so on. As I looked toward the diving board, who do I see but my Uncle Joe. In his Communion suit. Uncle Joe was about five feet tall, but everything he owned was big-assed. I mentioned his Cadillac in earlier chapters—he got a new, bigger one every two years. He liked to smoke big cigars, and he liked living in his big house. He did everything *BIG*.

So here it is, Labor Day weekend, and he's standing by the pool in a white suit with white shoes. Really, all he needs to do is to kneel in front of the upended bathtub Blessed Mother Mary that Mikey-boy planted in the grotto, and he can be mistaken for one of the kids at Fatima.

"Hi, Uncle Joe," I call from across the pool. "Nice suit." It just popped out of my mouth, and I knew I'd better be careful because my head still hurt from the powder room swat.

"Thanks, but it's white."

Really? I hadn't noticed.

"It looks good on you, Uncle Joe."

"Thanks honey, but I have to be careful what I eat. Your aunt will kill me if I get a spot on it."

No shit, Uncle Joe. Aunt Tes is the queen of clean. You're dead meat if you even think of soiling it.

"There are lots of goodies to eat in the dining room, Uncle Joe. They want everybody to come in and start eating."

Now, I cannot really remember exactly how it went down, but somehow Uncle Joe's taste buds overpowered my aunt's warnings, and Uncle Joe found himself in front of the shrimp with the cocktail sauce. As he was dunking shrimp into the sauce and torpedoing them into his mouth like B-52s, a big glob of red cocktail sauce plopped onto the front of his Communion suit. I swear this is the truth. The *world* went *silent* for about three seconds before my Aunt Santa says, "Ooooh Joe, let me fix it before my sister kills you." And she grabs a cloth napkin and wipes downward and up.

It looks like a big, red "J" on the front of the suit.

I cannot contain myself, because all I'm thinking of is Hester in *The Scarlet Letter.* Uncle Joe's letter could stand for "Joe" or even "Jesus," since he's certainly about to be crucified. My Aunt Tes has made Uncle Joe a plate, and he now must sit outside on the patio, shamed with his scarlet "J" for everyone to see, thanks to the help from Aunt Santa.

The cocktail sauce ruined Uncle Joe's suit, but it was the best cocktail sauce I'd ever eaten. To this day, I cannot make shrimp with cocktail sauce without thinking of Uncle Joe and his Communion suit.

I asked the fishmonger for the recipe. Use Uncle Joe as a cautionary tale, and don't wear white when you eat it.

Eat-with-a-Bib Shrimp and Cocktail Sauce
Serves 3 to 4 as an appetizer

1 pound *fressshhh* (is there any other kind?)
jumbo shrimp, cleaned

Boil shrimp until pink. Let cool.
Refrigerate until ice cold.

The Fishmonger's Cocktail Sauce:
    1 cup ketchup
    1 *fresshhh* (okay, I had to) lemon
    6 to 8 tablespoons horseradish (I like to use
        the hot prepared horseradish in a jar)

Mix the horseradish and ketchup and squeeze the
juice of one lemon into it.
The easiest recipe ever, with the best results.

Chapter 23: Fried Dough and TV Dinners

Winters in Upstate New York, when I grew up, meant you got yourself outside to shovel (no one had a snow blower), put the chains on your tires, and got your fat ass off to work. Even the school busses wore chains, and in order not to freeze to death waiting in a blizzard for the school bus, you waited inside and *listened* for the bus to come clanging down the road.

We never had a "snow day" off, the way we do now. Instead, kids looked forward to playing in the snow during recess in the school yard, and to sledding on Saturday and Sunday .

Our day was Sunday. My friend Ellen and I would suit up like Randy in *A Christmas Story*, then drag our sleds and /or toboggans almost two miles in six feet of snow to get to where the good hills were. All of that exercise got the appetite working. As Ellen tells it, I wasn't interested in food the way she was, and so my mom would invite her over to our house to eat because I was not a good eater and very skinny, and I would eat better if I had a friend to eat with. I can tell you, fifty years later that's certainly not the case. I don't care who's around; I just like to eat.

Anyway, after being in ten-degree weather for six to seven hours, we would drag our sleds/toboggans back the two miles to my house, where we would be greeted with fried dough and hot chocolate. Mom always made fried dough. She'd just make up some pizza dough and let it rise, then break off pieces to put into the pot filled with oil. All winter long our house smelled like grease because the adults never opened windows in the winter.

"Don't open that window! We'll all get pneumonia!"

"But Mom, we've been outside in the freezing cold all day."

"That's different!"

"How?"

"It's outside."

They would also pull the same kind of bogus story when we went down the shore. You know, the myth where kids couldn't go into the water for two hours after lunch or they'd drown. It took me twenty years to figure out why the adults told us that. So they could sit in peace and smoke and drink and not have to keep an eye out for us in the ocean. I know this to be true, because when I told my kids the same thing years later, they looked at me like I was nuts, and told me that that was an old wives' tale. Smart-asses.

But, I digress from the fried dough story. The fried dough would be served with powdered sugar and/or honey if you preferred. Hot chocolate would be on the table, and mom would put marshmallows in it.

It was such a wonderful treat for us, and when my kids were growing up, I sometimes did the same for them. However, I always open the windows whenever I fry something, which isn't often.

Now, while Ellen loved coming to my house to "help" me eat, I couldn't wait to get my ass over to *her* house for TV dinners. Her mom was no cook. To hear Ellen tell it, there were things that had been living in the refrigerator for twenty-plus years. She wasn't exaggerating, either, because we found a bottle of ketchup from a store that had been closed for twenty years. Mrs. Roberto was all about "waste not, want not."

So naturally Mrs. Roberto's signature food was TV dinners. Specifically, Swanson. I LOVED going over there for a nice hot TV dinner. She would let us choose the ones we liked from the grocery store. I was partial to the turkey dinner, which had turkey, gravy, mashed potatoes, cranberry sauce, and succotash, nicely sectioned in its own area. Underneath a specially wrapped section was an apple pie. Yum, yum,yum!

The beauty of it was that Mrs. Roberto would let us heat the oven and put our dinners in, all by ourselves. We had a *responsibility,* and this took place before microwave ovens. When the TV dinners were done (I do remember that they took forever to cook in the oven) we took them out with hot mitts and then proceeded to the living room to watch TV while we ate. Good God, how I loved going over there. Never once did Mrs. Roberto say, "Don't spill that" or "Be careful." No, she left us *alone.*

Sometimes, during legal holidays when we had no school, she'd take us on adventures. Once we went to a shrine in Auriesville, New York. We bought sandwiches from a Deli and ate them on picnic tables at a NYS Thruway rest stop. What a treat. Sandwiches that you *bought*! It's amazing what fond memories I have of something as simple as a sandwich.

However, the greatest adventure that Mrs. Roberto ever took us on was during the fall to the Old Cider Mill, several miles from our homes. They truly made cider at this mill. They also served up cider donuts, and to this day, no matter where I travel, I cannot find any that tasted like those. They were beyond flavorful. They were not on ANY weight loss diet plan, not now, not EVER, but they were in a class by themselves. Fabulous.

Well, anyway, the doors to the place were huge and latched, just like in a horror film. The old woman who owned and ran the joint was always there to greet you. You'd knock on the door, and she'd appear, all witch-like and scary looking. Quite frankly, it wasn't until years later that I found out that she ALWAYS looked like that; it wasn't a costume.

She'd pull open the door, and you'd step inside. And then the fun would begin. The place looked like a taxidermist's workshop. Every conceivable animal (dead, of course) was either displayed on all fours, mounted on a wall, or sitting on a table. And it was dark in there, too. As your eyes adjusted, you could see a whole moose standing to the right of the doors, and many raccoons with green glass eyes lined up on the tables. There were dead *somethings* pickled in formaldehyde. Foooooky is all I have to say.

But the real reason we would go there was for the cider and donuts. The family still owned the orchards behind the building, and they used their own apples to make the cider. As my memory serves me, we'd drink up several glasses and eat a few donuts and then… well, I can never remember the rest of what we did. I only know that for years we'd make our pilgrimage across the river and down a few blocks to the Old Cider Mill, which was in the middle of a residential area, but seemed like it could have been set in a Grimms fairy tale. And the eerie thing is that we could only remember going IN, never going OUT.

Many years later, with two children of my own, I would drive past the cider mill and remember all the great times I had there. Kind of like when you go back to visit your old college town and remember that wonderful bar…

The Old Cider Mill is one of the best memories I have of Mrs. Roberto. She loved the place as much as we did.

Today I make a mulled cider here at my house for the holidays, and always at Halloween. I like to close my eyes and pretend that I'm back at the Old Cider Mill, drinking cider while eating a cider donut, with the moose looking down on me ever so sinisterly. It's a comforting memory. Thanks, Mrs. Roberto.

Gloria's Mulled Cider Mill Cider:

One quart apple cider
One quart inexpensive dry sherry
One tablespoon whole cloves
Three cinnamon sticks
2 apples, cut and cored into wedges

Throw everything into a large pot and simmer all day. Ladle out as needed.

Chapter 24: My Big Fat Dysfunctional Italian Wedding

As I've said before, this bunch thrived on drama. So when I announced my engagement to my Hubby, well, think of the Roman Inquisition of the 14th century, fast forwarded to the Jersey Inquisition of the 20th century.

"We are having an engagement party, right?"

"Little Herbie had his at the Country Club."

"The Luzzos had theirs at the Willowbrook."

"Cousin Wayne had a big summer house party down the shore. Three hundred people at the Breakers and they served lobster, too."

"Michael had that fountain of booze, remember? You just put your glass under it, Remember? I had about fifteen of them gin and tonic ones. Delicious. *Delicious.*"

"Mindy, why not do it here? We'll bring."

"Is his mother Italian?"

As always, these questions came rapid fire. All of a sudden I was on the witness stand, a deer in the headlights. They were *crazy!*

I nixed the engagement party, which seemed like a good idea, but they made mischief about that anyway, putting in their two cents and calling my mom every chance they got, thereby driving both of us mad.

I had a year to plan, decide, and execute. Time was on my side, and soon all the wedding lists were complete. All that needed to be done was to wait for the response cards and make the guest list.

And that's where it got fooky.

The Jersey crowd doesn't believe the rules apply to them (see the chapter on picking gardunes from lawns). They certainly were not going to RSVP a yes without calling first to see where they would be seated. Since they all expected they would be able to sit where they wanted, they had no problem voicing their requests.

" Don't sit me at the same table as 'THE JANE.' Don't you remember how she treated Mama after Nick left? I will never forget it."

"Dick? Are you kidding me? I can't sit at his table. The thief stole my reading glasses at your house last Christmas. Put me there, and I won't come."

" Anthony? You want me to sit with that pig? No $&@/ way. He chews like a cow and spits all over the table. I should die first."

I was appalled by their requests. I always sat where I was assigned at weddings. After all, who cared where you sat? With free drinks and chow, it was a no brainer.

But the Jersey crowd stood firm in their requests. Though my mother was beside herself, I wasn't worried.

"Mom, who cares?" I said.

"I care!"

"But why, they won't even remember they were here." (Well, that wasn't exactly true. My cousin Elaine pitched a fit because I told her to put her double-wide pocketbook down for my sister's wedding pictures. She held on to it like her virginity. She was pissed off and didn't speak to me for a whole twenty years.)

So mom made tables for two and for twenty-two, till the seating arrangements looked like a McDonald's designed by the architecturally challenged. With that drama at bay (oh, but wait, there's more) I had to get to the task of dealing with the in-law, I mean, *outlaw* drama. Hubby's family legitimately consisted of four people, but my mother out-law wasn't going to be up-staged by the bride's side of the aisle, so she invited everyone she had ever come into contact with in her adult life. I do believe she didn't even know the last names of some of the losers she invited.

I pleaded with soon-to-be-hubby to give her a cut-off number, but no, we couldn't disappoint the mama. So I decided to get revenge another way—I *combined* some of my family with her guests at tables. Genius!

Be careful what you wish for.

Now, a big fat Italian wedding needs food, right? Mom had arranged for all of the typical reception fare, including the Venetian hour. But she knew that wasn't going to be enough, by any means. What about the early arrivals? And those who were coming back to the house afterward? No, she needed more food. And that meant trays of food for the house. Pounds of cold cuts, trays of ziti and eggplant, mounds of cookies. There really was no changing her mind.

The big day arrived, along with more drama. Twelve cousins decided to rent a van and drive up from Jersey. Of course the van was loaded with booze and food, which they indulged in for the two-hour ride upstate. When they spilled out of the van at my mom's house for a potty stop before church, one of the booze bottles broke and spilled all over three of them. The other nine fools laughed so hard that one peed his pants. They sloshed and staggered their way into Mom's house, where the photographer was trying to make the Kodak moment work, despite the fact that the night before we had a tropical storm and not only were branches and debris strewn all over the lawn, but a tree had collapsed half of the porch. Beautiful.

The four booze-soaked cousins were soon looting through my parents' closets, looking for clean clothes, while the other eight dug into the trays of food. The photographer was beginning to melt down, so I shooed them out of the house and onto the half of the porch that hadn't collapsed. But before this happened, my soon-to-be-brother-in-law delivered our flowers. As I stepped forward to take the box from him, the heel of my wedding shoe got stuck in the heating grate on the floor. I took my foot out of the shoe, and he had to use a hammer to get it out of the grate, ripping the leather.

After a few pictures and reloading the van with slowly sobering cousins, we were off to church.

You'd think the drama would stop once we were at church, right? Think again.

For starters, the priest forgot Hubby's name and kept calling him "Louie" in a thick Italian accent. It was a Saturday Night Live skit. The sobered up cousins were quiet... only because they were sleeping, and cousin Herbie proved it by snoring. Meanwhile, the out-laws were throwing eye daggers at me because, well, just because.

Finally we were out of there. Hubby and I decided to forgo the usual pictures of the wedding party, heading instead to the local hospital, to visit a friend who couldn't make the wedding because he was in traction from an accident. In leaving, we turned a deaf ear to the priest who is screaming at us to come and sign the marriage certificate. It wasn't until twenty years later, when we needed it, that we found out we never had a wedding certificate. Had I only known...

The cousins. sobered up, were ready for round two, so they headed out to the reception. My brother-in-law (see the chapter on squirrel stew) was my mother-out-law's escort. (I told you I'd get revenge). After a few cold ones, he hit the ground like he had been KO'd by Jake LaMotta and the mama, all 285 pounds of her, bless her heart, picked him up like a speck of dust. Of course he gave her his favorite Wicked-ism, "Fuck 'em if they can't take a joke," before collapsing into her arms. Quite a touching scene.

With the cousins at the bar torpedoing hors de oeuvres into their mouths and washing them down with the free booze, the aunts and uncles were flitting from table to table, looking for name cards and switching out the ones they didn't want to sit with. So much for seating arrangements.

My mom, in the middle of a meltdown, was visiting the abovementioned groups, anyway, trying to make nicey-nice with everyone. The outlaw contingency was staying close to one another, so as to get all the gossip that's fit to print. Newlyweds Lou and Gloria were by the pool, guzzling champagne and trying to lose the drunken cousins who insisted on coming with us to our house to see, as they put it, "the action." I was already tired from this smiling, fun-filled day, and we hadn't even had the antipasti yet.

In the middle of this circus we were called in to do the Grand March, parading in front of everyone to the drum-rolling Loser Brothers Band. The lead singer, named Giuseppe (you cannot make it up) looked and sounded like Shecky Green at a low-budget Catskill resort. His toupee was tilted to the right, while his lazy right eye gravitated to the left. He'd already had a dozen or so clams oreganata, and I could smell his garlic breath as he belted out "Mack the Knife." Later, after he sang it ten times in four hours, I found out that it's his "signature" song. Why, I wouldn't have guessed.

As we descended the staircase, I took stock of the groups of seated freeloaders:

The old-timers seated at table # 2 are my aunt and uncle from California who are letting everyone in the place know it's their fiftieth wedding anniversary, while smiling with parsley-infused false teeth. My grand-mother Cracker flanks their left, while her brother, Uncle Jimmy, sits on their right. They've been digging into the free martinis, and they're a little sloshed. The California relatives have also let everyone in the free world and beyond know that they live in Beverly Hills, all the time eating like longshoremen back from the Bering Sea.

Uncle Herbie and Aunt Santa (remember Bon Voyage Gertrude?) are at the next table. Uncle Herbie's son, Herbie, Jr. was one of the party bus cousins who wet his pants, and at six feet two inches tall, he's wearing a pair of my dad's brown trousers, which in no way match his sharkskin navy Nehru jacket. I should also mention that my dad was a stretch at five feet nine inches. All Aunt Santa can manage to say is "OOOOOHHHHH, how pretty Gloria looks." Her teeth are red from the roasted peppers, a vampire on a rampage. Uncle Herbie leans in to kiss me, and he's got the clams oreganata disease. Good grief!

Lou and I make our rounds to the party bus table, where the festivities continue.

"SHUT UP! There's no way I'm going to take a picture with HIM! He looks like a cross-dressing circus clown in that suit."

"In my teeth? What is it? I don't feel it. Where? C'mon Lu, pick it out, will ya? Here, use my pocket knife."

"She is still carrying that huge purse?"

"They didn't serve the shrimp like at my Wayne's.

His was jumbo size. Wayne had enough shrimp for an army at his wedding. His father-in-law was connected."

"At James' wedding, they had king crab, remember? And they gave us bags to take it home. Junie and Lucille put it in the cooler, remember? They had it in the trunk and just filled it up, remember? And they gave them ice, too. Filet mignon, too. All you could eat and to take home. What a spread, what a spread! I'll never forget it. Remember?"

At that point, Hubby and I are exhausted from all the merrymaking, so we decide to ditch. But before we did, we meet up with my brother, all of seventeen and totally wasted. We tell him to keep his mouth shut as to our whereabouts and he agrees, but first he plants a very long, wet kiss on my husband's lips and says, "I love you Lou, you're the best."

It's going to be a deep burn for him tomorrow, but we don't care, 'cause we're out of there.

As we arrived home to the first night as a married couple, all I could think of was how much my face hurt from all of the phony smiling I did. We collapsed into bed, drained, and laughed ourselves to sleep about what we found in Lou's cumberbund.

A provolone-stuffed green olive.

Stuffed Olive a la Lou

One jar large green Italian olives (not the
    martini kind, and preferably pitted)
½ pound good, sharp provolone
Enough virgin olive oil to fill and cover the
    olives in the jar
One tablespoon dried oregano
One tablespoon dried basil
Dash red pepper flakes

Cut the provolone into tiny bits.

Stuff the olive with the provolone.

Put olives in a glass jar or glass container and fill
with olive oil, herbs and red pepper flakes (the more
you use the hotter the olives).

Let marinate for a week in the refrigerator.

Chapter 25: Roasted Pigs and Deer Dogs

Growing up in my family, summer barbeques meant you were going to eat lasagna, meatballs, antipasti, potatoes, broccoli rabe, salad, vinegar peppers, bread, you get the message. It also meant that Mom would "throw on a few hot dogs and hamburgers" to give it the outdoor barbeque flavor.

She would open the door leading from the dining room to the front hall and out to a large porch, where the picnic tables were set up. You would fill your plate in the dining room, then jockey your food and drink to the porch, where you could eat your "picnic" food. Of course, there were always those who wouldn't comply and would draw up a chair and belly right up to the dining room table, where they would invariably sit *smack* in front of something you wanted. Of course they did. Hell, they weren't going to go outside to fend off mosquitoes and killer bees. They were going to sit their fat butts right in front of the food.

My brother was the one who introduced me to the glorified barbeque known as the pig roast. Now, that's a real barbeque. He would hire these guys called pig roasters, supply them with all the beer they could drink and all the eats they could swallow. He would then invite everyone he knew, did know, or might ever know to bring a covered dish and join the party.

The pig roasters would show up at his house around five a.m. on the day of the party with their roasting oven, the roastee, and various marinades, and then they'd begin slow cooking the sucker. After the setup, they'd pop a top to toast the endeavor. Naturally, my brother would get out of bed to greet the unfamiliar dawn and see how things were progressing.

When the marinade got used up, they'd pour their beers onto the roastee, giggling as they slurred:

"Some for the piggy... (take a sip...) and some for me." Hilarious.

The guests would arrive at noon to begin digging into the covered dishes while the piggy cooked to perfection. Every salad imaginable was lined up in ice troughs that my sister-in-law thoughtfully brought out, so as not to poison the guests with salmonella. There were steamer trays with sterno burners underneath them, filled with hot foods like sausage and peppers, baked ziti, roasted potatoes, hot wings, some kind of meat... *wait!*

What kind of meat was that?

"Hey Michelle, what's in this pan?" I ventured a sniff, but couldn't decide. Rabbit? Venison? A lot of the guys were hunting aficionados, so it wouldn't be so unusual...

"It's deer dog."

Listen, everyone's had their face in a red solo cup since they arrived, me included, so I had every reason to believe I hadn't heard her correctly.

"It's a deer dog?"

"Yes, isn't it cool? Frank shot it in the backyard, thinking it was a coyote, and Kathy couldn't resist cooking it. You know how she is. But don't tell anyone, because they may not eat it if they know (you got that right, sister) and her feelings will be hurt. And you know how fragile she is these days. Don't tell, okay?"

Don't worry, your secret's safe with me. They'll commit my sorry ass if I get those words out. But I'm still curious as to what exactly a deer dog is, so I ask the obvious.

"Okay, Michelle, my lips are sealed. But what exactly is a deer dog?"

"Well, it looks like a deer and it acts like a dog, so I just called it a deer dog."

What did I say in an earlier chapter? You cannot make this shit up.

Recipe for Delicious Roasted Pig

Get the pig roaster guys to do it for you. Costs a little extra and you are guaranteed to enjoy it a whole lot more than if you did it yourself! However, I know that a LOT of beer is involved, in case you decide to make a go of it!

Chapter 26: Down the Shore

Okay, readers' pop quiz: What day was Aunt Columbia born? Right! Columbus Day! Congratulations, you've been keeping up.

Aunt Columbia and Uncle Angelo lived down the shore: Manasquan, New Jersey, to those who don't know the vernacular.

Uncle Angelo was short and stocky, and called "Stogie" by his wife, because he always had a pipe in his mouth, even though a stogie is a cigar. Go figure. As a kid, when I would see those statues of fishermen who looked like sea captains, I honestly believed that Uncle Angelo posed for the molds. No, really I did.

Aunt Columbia was rather tall and big-boned, with a plain face and a heart of gold. Their house was on the bayside, a sprawling ranch with a dock for boats and a large screened-in porch. Of course. The porch had a large table with seating for twenty people. Of course. The family would descend on Manasquan for two weeks every July, mostly to allow time for the gossip about those who didn't come down the shore, and a little beach time.

Adults got to sleep in bedrooms, and kids got to sleep wherever there was a space. All of the cousins would show up, not only out of respect for Uncle Angelo, but for the food. Even my cousin Arthur, who wasn't going to eat anything from the table, joined us. Now here was a kid who wouldn't shower for fear of going down the drain—his bath water had to be drawn for him, and then he'd get out before the plug was pulled. This crazy nut would sit on the sidewalk for hours and eat ants—yes, ants, but he cried if my aunt forced him to eat pasta and fish. With all of the wonderful foods that Aunt Columbia would make, he ate ants.

Aunt Columbia was like an old fisherwoman from days gone by. She'd wear capris (before they were fashionable) and rubber flip-flops while digging into the sand for clams and mussels. She'd make all of the cousins help her carry buckets filled with these mollusks to her kitchen, where the magic would begin. First, she'd scrub the shells with a wire brush. No surprise there. Remember, the aunts in Newark scrubbed the meat before they cooked it. Must have been a Marra thing. Then she'd throw them in salted water "to get the poop out," she'd say. Cancer, poop, whatever... they all washed everything that came into contact with your mouth.

While this was going on, her sisters-in-law, namely, my mom and my aunts, would begin preparing the rest of the meal. Tomato sauce, salad, sausage, pepper, all the usual suspects. Uncle Angelo made his own wine, and he bottled it in old glass Coca-Cola bottles. The shit was so dark that you couldn't tell the coke from the wine.

Now it was the kids' job to set the table, and Aunt Columbia would have one of the older cousins take the wine bottles to the table—four bottles of wine for the adults, and one bottle of soda for the kids. I should mention here that, although Aunt Columbia had a heart of gold, she was also a little slow. She had contracted meningitis as a child and it left her deaf and challenged.

It was inevitable that one day she would confuse the bottles and my cousin Billy would open a bottle of wine for us to drink.

And one day she does. "Hey guys, taste it! It's wine!" Billy gleefully calls out to the rest of us. Aunt Columbia cannot hear what he's said, and continues cooking in the kitchen. By now, five cousins are feeling rather boisterous and full of themselves, until one is high enough to do the unthinkable. *He doesn't respond to a question that Uncle Angelo asks him.*

His mother flies into the dining room like a crazed vampire.

"Did you answer your uncle?" THE DEATH STARE.

"Oh, did he say something?"

SMACK!! Billy is guilty of the epitome of disrespect, and when you punished one, you punished all.

To this day, whenever I am in that particular cousin's company and we are drinking wine, I fondly remember what happened next.

All of us were sent to bed with sore bottoms, but the biggest punishment was missing out on all of those clams and mussels that were just swimming in that delectable sauce. I always felt that my punishment was the harshest, because the room where my sister and I slept was right off the dining room, under a window overlooking the dining room table. I could see and smell the wonders of the sea, and it broke my heart that I wasn't a part of it.

There is a happy ending to this story, however.

We had only been there for two days when this incident occurred, so Aunt Columbia was more than willing to make the fish and sauce dish again. This time we behaved ourselves, and got to enjoy the morsels.

Being "down the shore" ended when I got a boyfriend, and then a job, and then went away to college, but the idyllic times that I spent there will live forever in my memory.

Down the Shore Dinner

A marinara sauce is the best with fish, because it's light. This recipe can feed 6 to 8, so measure accordingly.

3 cans crushed tomatoes (Scalfani would be the preferred brand)
2 tablespoons chopped garlic
10 basil leaves
1 bunch parsley
Salt and pepper to taste
¼ cup of inexpensive dry white wine
5 pounds Prince Edward Island or Maine mussels
3 pounds littleneck clams
2 pounds extra large shrimp
Two pounds Ronzoni # 9 pasta

Fry garlic, basil, and parsley in enough olive oil to coat the bottom of a large sauce pot.

Quickly add the cans of tomatoes (they will sizzle, but that's good) and then lower the sauce to a bubbling boil.

Add the white wine to the sauce. Let boil for 5 minutes and then lower the heat.

Add salt and pepper to taste.

In the meantime, scrub the mussels and clams and peel and clean the shrimp. Set the seafood aside.

Get a large pot of water and set to boil; do not forget to salt the water.

When the water starts to boil, add 2 pounds of pasta (we love Ronzoni # 9).

As that is boiling, throw ALL of the fish into the sauce and bring it up to a boil as well.

When the pasta is al dente (follow the package directions or, if you prefer, burn your finger while pulling one strand out to test), drain the pasta, place in a very large bowl, and top with the fish and the sauce.

Serve immediately with a wonderful crusty bread to mop up the sauce.

Chapter 27: Pick Me a Winner

I never could understand my family's love affair with sweet potatoes. I mean, I could see the relationship between Italians and their "gravy," their meatballs and lasagna, but *sweet potatoes*? I feel like they should only be eaten at Thanksgiving, or with a pork roast.

Nevertheless, this bunch LOVED their sweet potatoes. My mom often recounted her sweet potato story to us—that is to say, every time she cooked them.

"Mama would give me a nickel for school lunch, but I'd go down the street to the potato man and get a *freshhhhhh*, hot sweet potato right from the roast for two cents. Then we'd skip school and see a movie at the palace for three cents. That's what the matinees cost. And we'd eat them just like that."

She always ended the story the same way. *"Just like that,"* she'd say.

I couldn't fathom anyone giving up lunch for a sweet potato, but then again, I didn't grow up in hard times. Mom said sometimes she would save her three cents to build up her savings so that when Frank Sinatra was at the Paramount, she'd be able to skip school to see him. "We'd sneak in the back and the guy at the door would let us in," she would proudly say. "We'd never tell Mama because she would have killed us."

(You got that right, sister. Mama may have been four-feet-nothing, but she demanded respect.)

The way Uncle Tony loved *his* macaroni, and cousin Joey loved *his* coconut custard pie, and Nick loved *his* fruitcake, my Uncle Sal Loved *his* sweet potatoes.

"Pick me a winner, will you, B?" He always called my Aunt Bianca B, or Josephine, or Jaycee, and there were more names. They had so many nicknames that when my mom passed and the funeral director asked me the names of her siblings, I was hard-pressed to remember the real ones.

Well anyway, sweet potatoes should *never* be put piled on a platter. I'll bet you never knew that. It would totally ruin their flavor and substance. Oh no, for this bunch, sweet potatoes had to be delivered ceremoniously, one by one, to the vultures waiting eagerly at the table. I truly enjoyed a pure roasted sweet, as we called them at my mom's house. "Want a sweet?" my mom would ask each person seated at the table. And of course she would bring each potato individually to the person who requested, so as not to pile them onto a plate, lest they get mushy.

So while all the talking, noise, hand-gesturing was going on, you had to wait until you were asked if you wanted one. Uncle Sal would say every time he got one, "It's a winner," like it was a lottery ticket.

And then it would begin.

"You got a winner, Nick? How about you, you got a winner, Tony? I got a winner."

And the kicker was, they never put anything on the potato. You know, like butter?

150

In later years, my mom would cook at least a half-dozen or so sweets for as little as four people, because you would never know who wanted one. I would go to her condo once a week, and she would take the left-over half-dozen or so sweets and put them into a plastic bag for me to take home, all mushy and mashed together. Yum.

I still love a sweet potato hot and roasted from the oven, but I also like to make "special" sweets for company. Here's my recipe:

Special Winners
Serves 4 to 6

5 sweet potatoes
1 cup real maple syrup
1 stick unsalted butter
1 cup dark brown sugar

Preheat oven to 375 degrees

Roast sweets in the oven until they are soft to the touch.

Cut in half lengthwise and peel off skin.

Melt syrup, butter, and sugar together in a saucepan.

Pour melted mixture over the sweet potatoes.

Bake in oven again until just bubbling.

Serve.

Chapter 28: Beef Burgundy Blues

I am certain you have figured out by now that I've had a hot, longstanding, not so secret love affair with cooking. With all of our crazy family get-togethers over the years, it would be hard to get away with not liking food or cooking.

What you also need to know is that I've had an equally passionate love affair with entertaining. I would entertain my friends at my parents' house, in my small college apartment, in the first real apartment after that I rented after college—wherever there was a front door.

My life became gloriously happy when Hubby and I built our own home. I can remember having friends over for hot dogs, which was the only thing we could afford after paying the hefty mortgage payments we had. We always said that someday there would be more than hot dogs on our menu, and I'm delighted to say that that day did arrive.

Hubby and I decided one holiday season to host a New Year's Eve party. We invited something like sixty people, and beef Burgundy was on my agenda. Yes, it was expensive to purchase the meat, but it was a meal that could be stretched with the addition of rice. I also ordered an Italian Sub sandwich for that night, which was infinitely cheaper than buying enough cold cuts, cheeses, and bread to make individual sandwiches. Two entrees were minimum fare in those days, you always had to make sure there was something for everyone.

We sent out invitations by snail mail (remember life before e-vites?) and got resounding yeses from everyone. *(Put that pork chop in the window…)*

And then, drama struck. We had a wicked snowstorm that day, which rendered the roads impassable. That was okay, because the sandwich went into the fridge, while the beef Burgundy just got better with age.

We put the party off until the next day.

Then drama struck *again*. We began receiving phones calls from friends who were coming down with stomach viruses and couldn't attend. We gave them time to recover, and pushed the party out another two days.

I was a little worried about the sandwich AND the beef Burgundy, but Hubby assured me that both were okay because, as he put it, there was enough booze in the burgundy to pickle it, and as for the sandwich, deli meat keeps for a week. Okay…

The party absolutely needed to happen on the final date, and it did. We were down about twenty people, but that meant more eats for everyone. At the end of the evening, as people were leaving, we tried to push the sandwich and the beef Burgundy into our guests' hands, but no one was taking. I think the fear of the virus was just too great—some of our guests who had been sick and were now feeling better had been digging into the food, and those who were well wanted to keep it that way.

However, my friend Gary, who is a wonderful cook, offered to take some of the beef Burgundy. I was ecstatic, and put the entire amount into a large Tupperware for him to take home. Now readers, remember Cracker's Tupperware chapter? Well, Gary did something not so far removed. Six months later I'm at his house, and he says:

"Hey Gloria, I'm not finished with your Tupperware, but I'll get it to you as soon as I am."

"No problem, Gary. If you need it, just use it."

"Well, I'm not finished with the beef Burgundy."

There is a silence that actually still resounds in my ears.

"What do you mean, you're not finished with it?"

"Well, I am still eating the beef Burgundy. It's really delicious, too."

He sees my confusion, and explains, "Oh, what I've been doing is taking it out of the freezer and sticking it into the microwave to defrost it—there's so much of it and I can't eat it all, so I scrape off some from the top and put the rest back."

OMG.

Gary was, is, and will always be a bachelor and God takes care of them because, well, because. I will certainly share more Gary-in-the-kitchen stories and his escapades in a later chapter.

However, here is my recipe for beef Burgundy or, as the French call it, beouf Bourguignon.

Recycled (Again and Again and Again...) Beef Burgundy

This serves 12 to 16 people, so buy accordingly.

4 cups chopped onions
2 peeled and sliced carrots
1 cup unsalted butter and ½ cup oil
6 lbs. boneless beef (half chuck, half rump)
    cut into one-inch cubes
½ cup flour
1 teaspoon salt
½ teaspoon black pepper
½ teaspoon thyme
½ cup brandy
2 cups beef broth (canned is fine)
2 cups California Burgundy (or New York, or
    whatever)
1 to 1 ½ lbs. sliced white mushrooms
¼ cup unsalted butter to brown mushrooms
Cooked rice

Preheat the oven to 325 degrees.

Sauté the onions and the carrots in ½ cup of the butter and oil in a heavy, deep, 12-inch skillet. Remove vegetables and reserve.

Add remaining fat to pan. Dredge meat in mixture of flour, salt, pepper, and thyme. Don't brown all the pieces at once, so as not to crowd the pan. Make sure all pieces are well-browned. This will take some time, so don't hurry it.

When all the meat is browned, return it to the skillet. Warm the brandy, ignite it, and pour it over the meat.

Then turn the meat into a large earthenware casserole or roasting pan. Pour the broth into the skillet, scrape up all of the good browned bits of meat, and pour over the beef.

Add the vegetables and wine. Mix well and bake in the oven for 4 to 5 hours.

Brown mushrooms in butter and add to the casserole, heating up for ten minutes more.

Serve over fluffy rice.

Chapter 29: Nancy, Ambrosia, and Toilette

The reason our crowd all knew each other, or at least knew *of* each other, is that we lived in a small town mostly made up of Italians who came *upstate* to get out of the cities.

Take, for instance, my friend's family who emigrated from Brooklyn.

Mr. and Mrs. came upstate with the Mrs.' mom and dad, aka "Grandma and Grandpa OOOOOOHH-HH." That's what we called them, because whatever you said to them, they'd respond with "OOOOOOHH-HH." Don't ask.

Their house was always in a state of confusion, and this was largely due to my friend Arlene's dog, Toilette, whom they all called Toy. He was a white toy poodle who could scare off burglars, copperhead snakes, and pit bulls. He was fearless as he'd wrangle snakes from their nests and toss them into a million pieces. The response from Grandma and Grandpa would always be... you guessed it... "OOOOHHHHH." Burglars never bothered because they had cased the house and had seen Toy in action. Wasn't worth it.

He had a place of honor in the tiny kitchen, tethered to a short leash that was tied to the refrigerator handle. Now, the Mr. and Mrs. lived in this apartment (the Grandparents OOOOHHHH lived on the other side of the house), and the Mrs. was a magnificent cook. On Sunday mornings you could find her in the kitchen, frying up the meats for the sauce, making braccioles and meatballs, and simmering homegrown tomatoes.

Toy would always be by the refrigerator, trying to stretch himself to the stove to get something that could possibly have fallen. If you even talked to him, he'd growl, ARRRRGHHH, and the Mrs. would scream at the top of her lungs.

"Shut up! You no good son of a bitch, SHUT UP!" This would make Toy all the angrier and he would do his growl, and the Mrs. would scream at him some more. It was a great way to spend the Sabbath.

The Mrs. made one dish that my family did not make: ambrosia. It was divine, as its name implies. Whenever they had a family event, which was every Sunday, she would make it. My sister and I loved her ambrosia, because she included maraschino cherries. We were all about the maximum red dye # 15 in our veins.

So, one Sunday I went over for my visit. Mrs. was in the kitchen in her uniform (hair rollers and housecoat) frying up the meatballs, and Toy was sitting by the refrigerator, getting ready to do the growl. I do not know how or when it occurred because it happened so fast, but somehow Toy got a piece of meat meant for the sauce, the Mrs. screamed, Toy growled, and the next thing we know she picks him up, leash and all, and throws him out the back porch door, where he flies through the air with all fours splayed and the grandparents saying "OOOOHHHH" as the Mrs. is screaming, "You no good son of a bitch! Drop dead!"

Toy lands on top of his dog house, which promptly collapses, and we wait with bated breath to see the result—Toy standing up and growling "AARRGGH-HH" at the Mrs., completely unscathed.

You can't make it up.

Toy is gone now, Grandma and Grandpa OOOOHHHHH are gone, the Mr. and Mrs are gone, but I still have the famous ambrosia recipe:

In the Dog House Ambrosia
Serves 8 to 10

2 20-ounce cans of pineapple chunks
1 11-ounce can of mandarin oranges
1 large (24-ounce) can of fruit cocktail
2 cups mini marshmallows
1 7-ounce bag of shredded coconut
16 ounces of sour cream
1 small jar of maraschino cherries (save some
    cherries for garnish)
1 cup crushed walnuts
1 cup *freshhhhhh* (she said it like that, too)
    whipped cream

Drain all fruit thoroughly. Mix the fruit with the sour cream, coconut, and marshmallows in a large bowl.

Important: Be sure all liquid from the fruit has been drained before mixing.

After all is blended, fold in the whipped cream.

Top with chopped nuts and garnish with remaining cherries.

Chapter 30: Emma, Margie, and Tony Potatoes

While I am on the subject of immigrants from Brooklyn, let me introduce you to two sisters and their brother.

Emma and Margie worked in the garment district in Manhattan, sewing peignoirs. Whenever any of us got married, we got the "peignoir set," a nightgown and bathrobe that could never be worn in real life. They were both made of stiff lace and layers upon layers of see-through chiffon and ALWAYS in white. During the bridal showers, everyone would "ooh and ahh" at the workmanship, and then the peignoir set was put away in the hope chest for many years, until it disintegrated from no use.

But that isn't the story here. The story is about these three siblings who came "upstate" only on weekends, where all they did was cook for their brother, Tony Potatoes. Tony didn't do anything. As far as anyone could tell, he didn't work, and had no intention of working, now or ever. Margie and Emma doted on him as if he were Jesus Christ himself. Whatever he felt like eating, they made whatever he wanted, no matter how tired they were or how late they came home.

In my observation, Tony had a great gig, and he was working it like it was his job.

Tony loved his potatoes, especially in a frittata with peppers and onions. If that's what Tony felt like, that's what the sisters made him.

When supper was ready, they'd call to him from upstairs, "Tony! Tony Potatoes! Dinner!" He'd be in the family room watching TV, and would slowly make his way up the stairs, acting all reluctant and disinterested, when in actuality he was salivating and couldn't wait to sit his lazy ass down for a meal.

It's obvious Tony got his nickname from loving potatoes. Thank God he didn't like Goulash!.

Here is the recipe for Potato Frittata. You can substitute asparagus for the peppers when it's in season.

Frittata for Two a la Tony Potatoes

Two baking potatoes cut into thin slices
One small onion, sliced thin
One green pepper, cut into strips
4 eggs, beaten
¼ cup olive oil
Salt and pepper to taste

Heat a large skillet and drizzle olive oil in the pan, adding the potatoes and onions. Cook until they are browned, and then add the peppers.

Cook peppers until they are just a little soft.

Pour the eggs on top of the mixture in the pan, turning the eggs until they are cooked to your liking.

Add salt and pepper and enjoy with a nice hunk of Italian bread or, better yet, put the frittata on the bread to make a sandwich.

Chapter 31: Dumpster-Diving Cookies

"No!!! Don't throw them out!"

Remember Gary of the everlasting beef burgundy? Well, that bachelor would refuse to throw any food out, even charred cookies that had adhered to foil.

During the Christmas season, twenty or so years ago, one of my single girlfriends found herself the guardian of her young toddler nephew. She wanted to give him a Christmas resplendent with a trimmed tree, decorations, and presents, including, of course, homemade Christmas cookies.

The problem was, she couldn't cook, bake, or boil water. For real.

To compensate for her culinary shortcomings, she had yours truly go to her house with all of the ingredients, cookie sheets, cookie cutters, and utensils, to help her bake sugar cookies.

I began by showing her how to turn on the oven. "Wow, that's awesome"! she exclaimed, as I skillfully turned the knob to the right until it hit 350 degrees. Apparently, the last time she had seen an oven being lit was in 1962 at her parents' house, when her mother had to light the pilot with a match.

We set out to mix and roll out the dough, and then I showed her how to use the cookie cutters and sprinkle the sugar on top.

"These look just like the ones in the bakery!" she exclaimed.

Ooooooo-kay...

We put the first two cookie sheets in the oven, but because she had never used it, and I wasn't certain how long to cook them, we burned the first batch. She got a little despondent about pitching them into the garbage can, but I assured her that we had plenty of dough to make many more cookies.

And that's when Gary of the Burgundy rings the doorbell.

"Hey guys! Making cookies? Sweet! Let me help."

Of course, we do not mind having an extra pair of hands to help, and Gary is an artist, after all. He decides that our cookies need an artistic touch, so he asks for confectioner's sugar and food coloring, and begins to make frosting to decorate the cookies. Everyone is okay with this because he IS an artist and quite creative. He finishes the bag of sugar and goes to throw it in the garbage can, and it happens.

"What did you do?" He's almost apoplectic. "Oh my God, you can't throw these out! They're *good* cookies!"

And before any of us get the chance to stop him, he grabs the foil sheet out of the garbage and eats the charred cookies off the foil. As he's picking away at the crumbs and searching the garbage can for the other foil, he's mumbling, "You just can't throw these away.

They're *good* cookies. You just don't know what's good."
No Gary, we don't. But we do know that God will once
again take care of you.

He continued to look through the can, but didn't
find any more cookies. (Thank God.) And he did decorate the sugar cookies beautifully. After all, he is an
artist.

Not Sanford and Son Christmas Sugar Cookies

Makes approximately two dozen 2 ½ inch cookies

> ¾ cup unsalted butter, softened
> 1 cup sugar
> 1 large egg
> 2 cups all purpose flour
> 1 teaspoon baking powder
> ¼ teaspoon salt
> 1/8 teaspoon ground nutmeg
> 2 tablespoons whole milk
> 1 teaspoon vanilla

Preheat oven to 400 degrees.

Cream butter.

Gradually add sugar, beating until light and fluffy.

Beat in egg.

Sift together flour, baking powder, salt and nutmeg.

Add to creamed mixture, alternately with milk and vanilla, to form stiff dough.

Wrap in wax paper and chill for 2 hours, then, on a floured surface, roll out the dough until 3/16 inch thick.

Cut into shapes with holiday cookie cutters and place on ungreased cookie sheet. Bake for 6-8 minutes until golden.

Cool on wire rack. Decorate as you wish.

Since this recipe makes approximately 2 dozen cookies, I usually double it.

Chapter 32: Sergio Valente and Turkey

The circus antics surrounding our family's holidays did not always originate in Jersey, as I have said in previous chapters.

There was one Thanksgiving when we actually had real snow (about fifteen inches) and the Jersey clan couldn't make it upstate for the feast. My mom had purchased two twenty-six-pound turkeys from a local farm and was not about to freeze them.... what would be the point in doing that? So she decided to invite all of Millie's (of Millie Cake fame) family for dinner, since they lived locally. Millie was one of our usual suspects at the Christmas dinners, but not so much for Thanksgiving. In addition to Millie, there was Dick, her husband and local kleptomaniac (see the chapter on pocket lasagna later), her sister Rosie and her husband, Petey, her brother, Petey (don't ask), and of course her baby brother, Mikey.

Because they lived across the street, there was no need to drive, they could walk. This particular day they were trudging over the highway, making their way up the front lawn to Mom's house when Millie takes a header and lands flat on her back in the snow. Her red wig goes flying to the left, her never-leave-her-face sunglasses go flying to the right, and there she lay, still.

"Millie! Are you hurt?" screams Mikey.

"Oh, my poor sister, she must be dead," Rosie is moaning.

"Can I help you up?" This is her brother-in-law Petey's lame attempt to be nice.

"NO, just leave me here to die!" Millie cries out dramatically, closing her eyes for even greater effect.

Dad and Hubby shovel their way clear to Millie in order to help her up on her feet. She's heavy to begin with, and she isn't budging, so she's dead weight. My dad was convinced from that day on that she was the reason for his hernia.

For Millie's sake I retrieve the wig and the glasses, putting them back on her as best I can. She also looks like a cross-dressing circus clown, but no one's laughing out loud, since Millie was a Sybil kind of gal, and you never knew who was going to show up.

We have a brief discussion, standing there over her body, as to whether or not we should take Millie to the ER, and it is decided that I would. So I load Millie and her brother Mikey into the car, and set off slowly for the nearby hospital.

Imagine this scene as we enter the ER:

Millie with her RED wig and her Sunglasses askew, plus Mikey, wearing a two-toned toupee and resembling Mo of the Three Stooges. Wait, there's more. As if that were not enough, Mikey is wearing tight designer Sergio Valente jeans with black dress socks and black dress shoes. To top off his New York City couture, he's also wearing Millie's double-wide pocketbook across his chest. The nurses don't know what to stare at first, and it's even more difficult to stare while their eyes are rolling.

"Help! Please someone help my sister," whines Mikey, half-heartedly.

I was just about to call for a wheelchair when one of the nurses wheels one right in front of Mikey, who promptly plops himself into it. "I'm having chest pains," he wails and they quickly cart his designer-jean-clad skinny ass off to a triage unit. Millie is still standing, but another wheelchair comes rolling out for her. Millie is yelling from her chair as she's whisked away, "Get my pocketbook from Mikey. I've got things in there!"

As I head over to the triage unit, a nurse approaches me, holding Mikey's toupee in one hand and Millie's pocketbook in the other. I reluctantly take them both and mumble thanks while I keep my head down. Best not to make eye contact lest I am recognized some day when I may need the ER.

I enter the examination room to find Mikey hooked up to an EKG with his pants around his ankles and his socks (with garters) and shoes still on. He's completely forgotten about his sister, and now it's all about him.

"Call Alice, tell her it's the Big One," he pleads with me.

Now, Alice is the last person I need to talk to, ever. If I've heard once that she used to be a Rockette, I've heard it at least 1,000 times. Truthfully, she may have been a Rockette fifty years ago, but now she looks like a bloated madam in a cheap bordello. She has legs like tree trunks, and the body of an old apple tree. She's been divorced from Mikey for twenty-three years. Apparently, their son used to get between them in bed (literally) until he was eighteen.

"Okay Mikey, give me her number." My plan is to pretend to call Alice from a pay phone, and then pretend that there was no answer.

I call Mom instead.

"What's going on over there?" she asks. "Where are you? The turkey will be too dry to eat if you don't get here soon. Your father is starving. Petey and Rosie are eating all the biscuits. Petey V. ate the ass off the turkey I was saving for you. What's taking you so long? Dick's stealing the silverware and he ate all the cashews in the lazy Susan."

Mom's only worried about the meal. Of course she is.

The day did end on a good note. Shortly thereafter, Mikey and Millie were deemed fit to go home and eat the Thanksgiving meal Mom had prepared. The snow did stop and the sun came out just as I was walking across the highway to fetch Millie Cake for dessert.

I can only wonder what the hospital staff thought as they witnessed this show. I'm certain none of them had wanted to work on a holiday, and now they were infinitely grateful that they had. I am also certain that they probably couldn't wait to tell the others on the next shift what drama they had missed.

As for me, like I always say, *put the pork chop in the window and they will come.*

Every Thanksgiving we fondly remember that trip to the ER, as my sister and I carve out the ass of the turkey to share.

Chapter 33: Cousin Louie and the Mystery Meal

Not too many years ago, while I watched on TV as Little Tony got whacked because he had done the Soprano family wrong, I had a flashback while looking at the show's upstate scenery. The setting where the "whack" took place looked exactly like Cousin Louie's house on the Lake.

"Cousin" Louie lived with two women, Aggie and Sally. One was his wife and the other his sister-in-law—or was one his sister and one his wife? I never quite knew, actually, but the three of them were totally interchangeable when it came to titles and, let's be honest here, when it came to relationships as well.

Watching the dynamics among the three of them was like watching the US Open.

"Get 'em a drink, Sally!" Louie would growl when Dad and I showed up. "Aggie, what you got cookin'? Cripes, she's always got sumthin' on that stove. Never ready, *never ready*. ALWAYS COOKIN'!"

Louis would shout these last two words for effect.

Both women would then scream at him to shut up. This always made for a pleasant Sunday afternoon for a kid out with Dad. Louie was about five-feet-three-inches in his prime. He ultimately lived to be 104 years old (he did have the Cracker disease, after all). By the time he died, he was even more of a shrinky-dink of a man.

On the other hand, Aggie was HUGE. She was as wide as she was tall, probably five feet both ways. She invariably wore a dress that looked like a kitchen curtain with a dirty white apron over it. *Always.* Aggie spent all day, every day, cooking *something* on a stove that sat in a corner of the screened-in porch. When I went to visit, we were always directed to sit on the dilapidated, low couches and chairs on the porch. We never went inside the house. *Ever.*

You may want to know why we never went inside, but I don't know the answer. It was just the way it was, and this dysfunctionality was acceptable. Just remember the rest of this bunch... anyway, what was cooking all day, every day on the stove on the porch? Good question. It was a mystery, and because we were never offered anything to eat, I never did find out what was on the stove till much later.

Whatever it was, Louie would try to move it along. "Ain't it ready yet, Aggie? Huh? Never ready, always cookin', cookin'. Never ready. Cripes!" Louie was an orator of epic proportions.

Now, it's just as well we were never offered any of this mystery, because the smell from the stove was *awful.* Whatever it was, it might just as well have been old socks boiling. Seriously. Sally would periodically go over to the stove to cop a stir when Aggies's feet were too swollen for her to do it herself. The rest of their time was spent sitting on one of the worn couches covered in worn cloths.

With my child's mind I reasoned that the three of them never did eat at all, neither did they move much from their preferred seating. *Ever.* I also reasoned that they had no olfactory senses to be able to put up with the God-awful smell.

I periodically visited Cousin Louie with either my dad or Cracker, but as the years passed, those visits became mercifully less frequent. When my son was born, my dad thought it would be a good idea to visit Louie before he bit the big one. Hell, by then he was 102 and anything could happen. So the three of us, my dad, my son and I set off for the Lake one fall Sunday afternoon.

When we arrived, Louie was much shorter than I had remembered, but then he was shrinking rapidly. As I had remembered, there was no going any farther than the porch. The stove still stood in the corner, no longer in use.

"How 'bout a drink?" Louie asks us. I decline, because I figure that no good can come of this, but dad mumbles, "Sure." Louie walks over to his preferred seating, where there is a small table with a bottle of anisette on it. He grabs it and pours the liquid into two murky looking glasses.

"Salut."

"Salut." Down the hatch. I'm thinking Dad's going to be sorry, just as Louie is about to offer him another shot. Before he feels obligated to say yes, I pipe up:

"Hey, Cousin Louie, do you remember Aggie always cooking on the stove? I always wanted to know what it was that she was cooking." *NOT*, but I'm trying to spare Dad from being further poisoned, by deflecting a second drink with a question.

"Cookin'? Broccoli rabe. Why, what did you think it was?"

Broccoli rabe. Well, that explains the old sock smell, but when I cook it, it doesn't take all day.

Okay, here it comes.

"Hey Cousin Louie,why did Aggie cook it all day?" *Do I really want to know?*

"Ya gotta get the wildness out of it, or it will give ya gas. Back you up for days. Boiling it all day gets the wildness out."

I couldn't make this shit up for money.

Louie passed on at the ripe old age of 104, with many of my questions about him, Sally and Aggie left unanswered.

I think I make a pretty good broccoli rabe, so I'm sharing my recipe with you. Perhaps Sally and Aggie truly thought that boiling it was the answer. I think I know where they went dyslexically wrong. You'll see what I mean when you read my recipe:

Broccoli Rabe
Serves 3 to 4

One bunch of fresh broccoli rabe
Pot of salted boiling water
One bowl of ice water, set aside
Salt and pepper to taste
Two cloves garlic, minced
Two tablespoons olive oil
Italian bread

Place broccoli rabe into boiling water and let come back up to boil. Boil for 5 minutes.

Take out and immediately plunge broccoli rabe into ice water for 1 to 2 minutes. Drain.

For freezing, put into a zip lock storage bag.

If using right away:

Place the garlic in the oil and cook until almost brown.

Throw broccoli rabe into the hot oil and mix all together. Add salt and pepper to taste.

Cut a nice (all food is nice) chunk/hunk of Italian bread and place some of the broccoli rabe on it. *Eat just like that.*

FYI: Plunging broccoli rabe into cold water gets the "wildness" out. I guess Sally and Aggie forgot that step. We're only human.

Chapter 34: Pocket Lasagna

Only Millie would have married the handyman. And there's no way this guy would have been mistaken for the pool boy, take my word for it. Millie married Dick, the kleptomaniac mentioned in the previous chapter.

I don't know how to even describe him: short, gnome-like in looks, and child-like in his mannerisms, attracted to shiny objects. I guess that's as good a description as any.

Dick never stole anything of real value, although he was partial to things like silverware, reading glasses, and hair accessories—those kinds of things. Truly harmless, he was a good soul who just had a small larceny habit, that's all. Dick spent every Christmas holiday with us, so we got to know his procedures. After he'd case the joint, he'd go into the living room to lift any reading glasses left near the *TV Guide*. Next, he'd circle the Christmas tree, looking for insignificant trinkets—hair clips, ribbons, a cheap plastic toy. After those went into the large pockets of the coat he always wore, he'd then come to the dinner table, where he'd lift a small spoon or a butter knife. As we kids became older, we would actually leave stuff specifically for him, to see if he would bite. Yup, he always did.

One particular Christmas Day, as Mom is bringing the platters of food into the dining room, we were watching and waiting to see what Dick would lift from the table. Disappointment sunk in as we pass around our plates; he hadn't taken anything.

Yet.

Suddenly, I get kicked under the table. My cousin looks over at me, and then at Dick. Dick is laughing and talking with everyone, at the same time as he's calmly taking forkfuls of lasagna and *seeming to drop them into his lap*! No way! I am beside myself with glee. Is he really just dropping food into his lap? Isn't that messy? We can't tell what his plan is, but after dinner we begin a search. It didn't take long for us to find it.

Dick had taken off his coat before dinner and left it on the stair railing in the hall. As we search his pockets ("Pockets" was also the rest of the family's nickname for him) we find my mom's damask table napkin filled with lasagna! Of course we squeal on him, and Millie beats him senseless for stealing. Apparently, the motive was to feed their dog, Junior, when he got home. When Millie hears *that,* she beats him again. Junior wasn't supposed to get table food. Table food was for mere mortals. Millie cooked him *special* food. That dog was treated like a king, believe me. When Junior died, Millie got a *white casket* for him.

Well, every Christmas thereafter, and to this day, whenever we have lasagna we always stop and take time out to fake-recreate Dick's unique way of stealing lasagna.

My mom made great lasagna. Definitely worth stealing. I recently learned how to make *freshhhh* ricotta, which is the only way I make lasagna now. Here is the recipe.

Ricotta

6 cups whole milk
4 cups heavy cream
3 tablespoons white vinegar
1 teaspoon salt

Cook milk, cream, and salt on top of stove in a large heavy pot, stirring constantly. When the thermometer reaches 190 degrees, turn stove off and add 3 tablespoons of white vinegar.

Let sit for 10 minutes, then pour into cheesecloth draped over a large bowl, vessel, or whatever you have. The whey will separate from the curd and will yield about 3 cups ricotta. If not using immediately, refrigerate.

For the uninitiated, curds are the part you eat. Whey is the liquid by-product. My brother uses the whey instead of water when he makes dough for pizza.

Ricotta gets creamier the longer it sits, so try to control yourself and don't eat it too soon.

Chapter 35: It's Five O'Clock Somewhere (Earlier If You're a Senior Citizen)

Remember Cracker of the Healthy Dinners? Her family's mothership was all about an afternoon drink with a little something to eat. Cracker, Uncle Jimmy, and the whole crew of them loved their martinis at four. All it took was for one of them to say, "Is it four o'clock yet?" It never mattered if it was or not. because Uncle Jimmy would take out the gin, the jar of olives, vermouth, the glasses, ice and shakers anyway, just because the question came up. Then the mixing and shaking would begin. Cracker liked hers dirty, Uncle Jimmy liked his dry, and Aunt Kitty (remember the Beverly Hills contingency at my wedding?) just plain liked them.

Wherever they were—Beverly Hills, Florida, New York City—at four o'clock, it happened. And wherever they were, someone would go to the fridge and take out the old Cracker Barrel cheese and a few Triscuits for munching. In between munches, they would all light up a smoke. Is it any wonder each of them lived to be 100, 96, and 103 respectively? No shit, there had to be something to this lifestyle, and I was damned if I was going to miss out on their longevity secret.

Hubby and children and I went to Florida one spring break to find out exactly what the secret of their boozy fountain of youth was. Well, we also went to Disney World with the kids as a side trip. On the plane trip going south, my son sat on my lap, crying the entire time with an ear infection. The kind stewardess (now there's an oxymoron) tried to make him happy by feeding him endless chocolates. The trouble was, they were the same ones she was handing out to the liquored-up fools in first class, and guess what they were filled with?

Needless to say, my child on overload promptly throws up all over me.

Between the curdled-milk-smelling puke and the chocolate liquors, I now smell like a bar in downtown Cleveland. As I return to my seat after trying to clean up in the miniscule bathroom, the other passengers are ill-grilling me as I waft down the aisle. I have my pride, though, so I hold my head up high as I return to my seat.

The plane finally lands—not soon enough for the other passengers, I'm sure.

Uncle Jimmy is there to meet us with his big-assed Lincoln. We load the luggage, two car seats, portable crib, two strollers, diaper bag, both kids and ourselves into Uncle's car. I get in the back seat, where even I can hardly stand the way I smell.

Uncle Jimmy: "Jesus, what the hell happened to you? Get drunk on the plane? You smell like a bar in downtown Cleveland."

The next day, as it approaches four p.m., Uncle Jimmy sounds the alert.

"Is it four o'clock yet? *Martini time.*"

As if on cue, the zombies walk from the patio to the kitchen, removing the Cracker Barrel from the fridge and the Triscuits from the pantry as Uncle Jimmy takes out the gin, olives, vermouth, shaker, glasses, and ice. He begins to make a dirty martini for Cracker, a dry martini for himself, and whatever for Aunt Kitty. He then asks hubby what he'd like. I say, "Hey Uncle Jimmy, what about me?"

Without missing a beat he says, "After the drinking you did on the plane? No booze for you!"

You know the kicker? There wasn't any fountain of youth mystery, after all. They were just pickled, that's all. And pickles last forever. Mystery solved.

Who cares that they wouldn't share their spoils with me? I never liked gin anyway, so I am sharing my love of Campari with you in what I think is the best summer drink. Ever. And the best part is, it doesn't get you pickled.

No, Virginia, we're not in Margaritaville Campari with Soda
Makes one drink

Lots of ice in a tall glass
One shot of Campari
Club soda
Lime

Pour club soda over ice and Campari.
Serve with lime wedge.

Chapter 36: Brussels Sprouts and M&Ms

When I went to college in upstate New York, we really didn't do the dieting thing. I think the weather may have had something to do with it. It snowed from the end of August to May, so you needed that extra padding to see you through those long winters. Or maybe we just were a lean group of girls who didn't need to diet.

Anyway, long before Jenny Craig, Lean Cuisine, and so on, our friends on Washington Street were the diet queens. If ever you wanted to lose a few pounds, the trick was to just *visit* them. You didn't need to do anything special.

Why, you ask?

Well, the smells that came from their kitchen were unreal. You see, they thought dieting meant eating lots of vegetables, and to their way of thinking those vegetables should be boiled. In one pot. All together, until they cooked down. Only then could they be eaten.

I would actually have to hold my nose to go there, no lie. Often I'd make excuses because I couldn't stand the smell.

One time one of them was boiling brussels sprouts.

The stench permeated the entire upstairs apartment, the downstairs apartment, and several blocks south.

So you see, just going there would make you not want to eat, and therefore *their diet* became *your diet*. Simple.

That is, all except Saturday nights, when all bets were off. That was party time on Washington Street. There was no boiling anything on that night. Serving bowls filled with M&Ms were placed on every flat surface in the apartment. Barbeque potato chips and cheap canned onion dip were right alongside them. And that's all. They were poor, too. Everyone would load up on chips and dip for dinner, and save the M&Ms for dessert.

Oh, I forgot the most important thing: drinks. Boone's Farm Apple Wine was the drink of choice for the ladies. We couldn't afford anything else and we felt really grown-up drinking *wine*. We lived twenty minutes away from the Genesee Beer Factory, and the guys drank Genesee (Genny for short) Cream Ale like it was their job.

When Sunday rolled around, you could find most of the guys sprawled on the living room floor, ashtrays filled to overflowing, pyramids made from Genny cans wherever there was space.

Then The Boiling of the Brussels Sprouts Ritual would begin. This was the signal *to get out immediately* or asphyxiate and die.

I think the dieters on Washington Street actually had a sweet deal going. Eat /drink green water all week and then party it up one night out of seven. It worked;

they were all svelte within a year. Not that I'm ever going to try it. I'm just making an observation.

Whenever I remember those times, I often laugh about the brussels sprouts. A few years ago I found a recipe for brussels sprouts and, never having known any other way to cook them but boiled, I gave the recipe a whirl. Everyone loved them, and they have become a family favorite.

We Don't Eat No Stinkin' Brussels Sprouts
Serves 4 to 6

1-½ pounds brussels sprouts, washed and cut
  in half
6 slices bacon
2 thinly sliced shallots
Salt and pepper

Fry the bacon in a heavy skillet, removing bacon when crisp.

Drain bacon on paper towels.

Put shallots and brussels sprouts in the same pan with salt and pepper, stirring continuously as the sprouts get brown and a little softened.

Crumble the bacon on top of the sprouts, sprinkle with salt and pepper, and serve.

Chapter 37: Fon–due You?

It seems like everyone who got married in the '70s got a least one fondue pot as a gift. I was lucky and got two. (I also got five cheeseboards with cheese-cutting knives and six sets of wine glasses with decanters... remember them?). They always say, "Keep your old stuff and wait for the fashion to return." Well I didn't and it did, against all odds. Fondue has made a comeback, featured in restaurants like The Melting Pot. Who'da thunk it?

After life in college, most of us grew up, got married, and set about the task of learning how to entertain. We had a great beginning, too, with all those wine glasses, decanters, and cheese boards.

Here's a memory-jogging blast from the past:

The Sexy Seventies Wine and Cheese Party

Go to the liquor store, buy a bottle of Mateus wine and pour it into one of the decanters. Then melt a candle end and stick it into the top of the empty Mateus bottle. Place it proudly on the huge cable-spool coffee table that you begged the phone company to let you have, and that you sanded down and polyurethaned with five coats of the carcinogen-in-a-can.

Next, buy some blocks of "fancy" cheese, say white Cracker Barrel and the gouda with the red rind—that's always a classy touch.

For the crackers, forget the Ritz and Saltines... they're far too common. Buy some Triscuits. Your guests will be impressed to see you're living large.

Invite your newlywed friends over for Friday night, since no one wants to miss SNL on Saturday.

Does any of this sound familiar to you, readers?

My yuppie (I guess that's what we were called) friends, I and hubby-to-be entertained this way at our house or the house of one of our couple friends every Friday night until the kids arrived. That was the end of all those wine glasses, decanters, and cheeseboards.

However, I have really digressed from the fondue!

Since everyone I knew had been given a fondue pot at one time or another, we would have fondue parties at each others' homes periodically. Now, most everyone was STILL POOR from college, so cheese seemed to be the likely choice for dinner in the fondue pot.

We all tried to outdo each other with different cheese recipes.

We had the "basic" fondue with Gruyere, and the "beer" fondue with... Genny Cream Ale, what else? We had the three-cheese fondue, and the list goes on and on. Our fondue parties had cheese and... bread cubes. No vegetables or anything else. Some of our friends would cut Wonder Bread into cubes and put them on a platter for dunking. The problem was that the bread would disintegrate immediately upon hitting the hot cheese, and then you would have to fish it out. And while you were fishing it out, it would sink deeper into the pot, to be happily reabsorbed into the cheese.

Some of the guests were double-dippers. They would dunk their bread cubes into the hot cheese and then put them into their mouths, biting off some of the cheesy cubes, and then *re-dunk* those cubes into the pot *again*. You could argue that the hot cheese kept the germs out of the pot, but I wasn't having it. So, once again, I would always do my dipping first, and after the first dunker began, I would be content with just bread.

Oh, and a glass of Mateus. Ah, the good old days!

I really do not care for fondue (wonder why!), but I did eat at one of the fondue restaurants. It was a three-hour meal, so that by the time I finished dessert, I was ready to eat again. Another reason I'm not a fan.

No surprise that I really don't have a fondue recipe, but I do have a nice recipe for baked Brie that goes well with any type of cracker, and could count as a fondue of sorts, since the cheese is served warm and melted.

Livin' Large Baked Brie

A nice piece of Brie cheese (8 ounces)
1 package Pillsbury Crescent Rolls
½ cup light brown sugar
¼ cup walnuts or pecans
¼ cup dried cranberries (optional)

Lay out the entire crescent roll package, forming a diamond shape with the rolls.

Place the Brie on top.

Put the brown sugar and nuts on top of the Brie with cranberries.

Fold the dough inward to create a diamond shape.

Place on an ungreased cookie sheet and bake until golden brown.

This is delicious with a really plain cracker, which allows the flavor of the cheese to come through.

Chapter 38: The Biscotti-Busters

Remember Aunt Gloria of the smiley-face cake? She would never serve my poor uncle a decent meal, because *she* was always dieting.

Uncle Frank was tall, thin, and an amateur golfer. He was also a really nice guy. Aunt G. would serve him white-bread bologna sandwiches, along with other food that wasn't quite as nourishing as it should have been, especially for a guy who spent the majority of his life on a golf course burning a kajillion calories. It's no surprise that he would drive to my parents' house in snowstorms just for dinner. He was *starved*.

We had a saying about people who looked under-nourished, as he did: "They need a good dish of macaroni." He needed to beef up. He needed *beef*.

When my daughter's about four weeks old, I get a call from Aunt Gloria:

"Hi Hon, are you home"? Seriously? *No, this is the answering machine, fool.*

"Yes, I'm home."

"Oh, your uncle just came back from having an EKG and all looks good, so he wants to take a ride and see the new addition to the family. Is that okay?"

Now, normally I love having company, but my aunt was a pain in the ass, plain and simple. Besides, with two babies under the age of two, there really isn't much in the way of treats in my house. And besides, I had no time to cook. So they're probably only going to get coffee, if I can find the coffee maker underneath the cans of formula.

"Sure," I say, after a gulp or two.

"We'll be there in a few."

I unearth the coffee maker and find some coffee. I debate stretching the creamer with formula. That would be shabby of me.

The doorbell rings. Aunt and Uncle enter and go right upstairs to the baby—Do Not Pass Go. "Oh, she's so cute! Look at that red hair, just like Grandpa's!" I'm thinking, *Yeah, yeah. Just look, don't touch, and get the hell out of here as soon as possible.*

But, somehow managing a smile, I'm saying instead, "Would you like a cup of coffee?" *Wait. What am I thinking? I just wanted this to be a drive-by visit, and now I'm going to make coffee.*

"OH, we'd love some." Of course.

"I feel terrible that I don't have a treat to go with the coffee, but I've been just a tad busy…" and as I am saying this, I look at the top of the refrigerator and there it is—THE TIN. Hubby's mama was no baker, believe me. Her idea of "baking" was to go to the supermarket and buy every different flavor of Entenmann's cheese Danish, Hostess chocolate doughnuts, and Freihofer's cookies. To her credit, she did admit to not being a baker.

However, in an effort to "do" Christmas cookies like everyone else, she made a batch of Italian biscotti that wasn't all that bad-tasting during the holiday, but the tin had been forgotten, and now it is the end of February and I only remember it when I see it. Fressssssh they are not.

"Hey," I say to my guests, "mama-out-law (okay, I said mother-in-law, but I was *thinking* the other) made some biscotti, and they may be kind of dry, but if you dunk them in the coffee..." And instantly poor Uncle Frank digs into them. As usual, he's *starved.*

I try one, but truthfully, I cannot bite into it. I have to use my back teeth to break a piece off, and there's no chewing it, really, you'd just have to soak it in coffee for the better part of an afternoon to make it even chewable. I'm all apologetic about the staleness of the biscotti, but Uncle Frank says, "These are delicious. I am really enjoying them!" And with that he eats about five biscotti.

Since I am not going to eat them, I wrap the rest in foil and give them to Aunt and Uncle as they take their leave, thanking me profusely for the delicious cookies, and promising to come back soon. Since the following day begins the Lenten Season, I already feel like I've done my Penance.

Two hours later, Mom calls. "I have some bad news." (Before I even find out what the deal is, I'm feeling vaguely happy, to be honest, because the worst kind of bad news usually means veal cutlets...)

"What?"

"Uncle Frank died."

"Like hell he did! He just left my house after eating the mama's stale biscotti."

"I know he was at your house. Listen to me. I just got off the phone with your grandmother. They got home and he said he wasn't feeling well and he dropped dead, just like that."

Can the mama be tried for murder, then? Now I'm really excited, but I feel badly for Uncle Frank. He was such a good guy.

For years afterward, I would periodically tell the mama-out-law that her cookies killed my uncle.

Give it some thought, and thanks for reading.

About the Author

Gloria Carnevale is the pen name of a teacher, wife, mother, writer—and cook—living in Dutchess County, New York, aka "Upstate."

CPSIA information can be obtained at www.ICGtesting.com
Printed in the USA
BVOW05s0419201114

375889BV00001B/5/P